ASHE Higher Education Report: Volume 35, Number 1
Kelly Ward, Lisa E. Wolf-Wendel, Series Editors

Bridging the Diversity Divide: Globalization and Reciprocal Empowerment in Higher Education

Edna Chun

Alvin Evans

#31 7456454

Bridging the Diversity Divide: Globalization and Reciprocal Empowerment in Higher Education
Edna Chun and Alvin Evans
ASHE Higher Education Report: Volume 35, Number 1
Kelly Ward, Lisa E. Wolf-Wendel, Series Editors

ISSN 1551-6970   electronic ISSN 1554-6306   ISBN 978-0-4705-2562-3

The ASHE Higher Education Report is part of the Jossey-Bass Higher and Adult Education Series and is published six times a year by Wiley Subscription Services, Inc., A Wiley Company, at Jossey-Bass, 989 Market Street, San Francisco, California 94103-1741.

For subscription information, see the Back Issue/Subscription Order Form in the back of this volume.

CALL FOR PROPOSALS: Prospective authors are strongly encouraged to contact Kelly Ward (kaward@wsu.edu) or Lisa Wolf-Wendel (lwolf@ku.edu). See "About the ASHE Higher Education Report Series" in the back of this volume.

Visit the Jossey-Bass Web site at www.josseybass.com.

Printed in the United States of America on acid-free recycled paper.

The ASHE Higher Education Report is indexed in CIJE: Current Index to Journals in Education (ERIC), Current Abstracts (EBSCO), Education Index/Abstracts (H.W. Wilson), ERIC Database (Education Resources Information Center), Higher Education Abstracts (Claremont Graduate University), IBR & IBZ: International Bibliographies of Periodical Literature (K.G. Saur), and Resources in Education (ERIC).

Advisory Board

Contents

Executive Summary

The sweeping forces of globalization present new challenges for higher education and research universities. This monograph documents major trends in globalization and then addresses how the external pressure of globalization demands transformation of university cultures to be more diverse and inclusive. Specifically, globalization has fostered an increasing emphasis on talent, creativity, and innovation, regardless of the historic barriers of race and gender. The dramatic increase in diversity among student populations coupled with the increasing demographic dominance of minority populations both at home and abroad represents a clear mandate for change. As a result, the university must create a system of higher education that develops the talents of all its members. As a result of the unfinished business of remedying the underrepresentation of minorities and women in higher education, our focus in the monograph is specifically on the achievement of a climate that supports the inclusion of minority and female faculty and staff. Put simply, the university cannot afford to waste human talent and the cultural and social richness that underrepresented groups bring to their campuses.

How do we transform the culture of higher education to respond to this new challenge? This monograph introduces the model of reciprocal empowerment as a core ideology that can counteract asymmetric power relations and promote the full participation of minority and female faculty and staff. Reciprocal empowerment is a values-based approach that consists of three powers: the power to define one's own identity *(self-determination)*; the power to give oneself and others adequate resources *(distributive justice)*; and the power to give oneself and others a voice *(democratic participation)* (Prilleltensky and

Gonick, 1994). Reciprocal empowerment and diversity are organizational "intangibles," just as talent, shared mind-set, learning, accountability, collaboration, and leadership are intangibles (Ulrich, 1998a). Recent research indicates that intangibles have a significant impact on both organizational success and the financial bottom line (Becker, Huselid, and Ulrich, 2001).

A multidimensional model based on demography, diversity, and democracy (Prewitt, 2002) provides a contemporary framework for the actualization of reciprocal empowerment and inclusion. This model expands on Florida's framework (2007) of the three T's (technology, talent, and tolerance) to identify democratic values, the rich diversity of the American landscape, and a compassionate, respectful campus environment as essential for institutional vitality and success.

Organizational learning represents the channel through which reciprocal empowerment can be transmitted to the institution. A central argument of the book substantiated by current research is that organizational learning is one of the most powerful levers for change in support of diversity. Reciprocal empowerment and organizational learning are transformative forces that can enable the university to respond to global needs and create inclusive environments. Organizational learning involves the capacity to create new mind-sets and mental models that will in turn lead to new institutional norms, assumptions, and habits (Argyris, 1993; Argyris and others, 1994). A systematic process of organizational learning helps to overcome internal resistance, reduces prejudice and bias, and creates new patterns of behavior and action.

Several key questions are addressed in this monograph: What are the primary drivers of diversity transformation? What are the principal areas of focus that need to be measured in an institutional assessment of workplace diversity? What organizational concepts pertain to the change process, and how can they be linked to research-based tactical approaches? What specific institutional practices, instruments, and tools facilitate organizational learning in support of diversity?

The book is designed as a companion to an earlier monograph, *Are the Walls Really Down? Behavioral and Organizational Barriers to Faculty and Staff Diversity* (Evans & Chun, 2007a) and moves from conceptual identification of barriers in the earlier publication to results-oriented action plans.

Developing an action plan for implementing an inclusive campus environment built on reciprocal empowerment links the institution's core values, culture, structural practices, and workplace processes to the outside world through the prism of diversity. This monograph includes concrete tools, measurement strategies, and best practices from public research universities designed to assist educational institutions in building a versatile and flexible repertoire of organizational approaches to reciprocal empowerment. Its focus is on research-based, practical strategies that will enable institutions of higher education to assess current practices and move beyond structural representation to reciprocal empowerment. Only by systematic organizational change will universities bridge the diversity divide and create an inclusive culture that values and celebrates the contributions of all its members.

Foreword

In 2007 Alvin Evans and Edna Breinig Chun authored an ASHE Higher Education monograph titled *Are the Walls Really Down? Behavioral and Organizational Barriers to Faculty and Staff Diversity.* The monograph used the concept of reciprocal empowerment to show how faculty and staff can work together to improve the climate for diversity in research universities. The monograph was given the Kathryn G. Hansen Publications Award at the College and University Professional Association for Human Resources national conference in recognition of its significant contribution in the field of human resource administration. The present monograph, *Bridging the Diversity Divide,* continues the discussion raised in their previous work and offers a natural next step in a solution-oriented approach to changing campus climate and culture to be more inclusive.

The present monograph frames diversity as important in light of global economic trends and the current political climate. Although this topic has seen a fair amount of lip service in recent times, it is also one that remains fairly underdeveloped because of the inability of colleges and universities to develop sustainable plans and actually follow through. In this light, the topic continues to be extremely relevant to current issues in higher education. The present monograph avoids the pitfalls of superficiality by being very clear as to how diversity and globalism intersect and reinforce one another in the context of higher education.

Evans and Chun root the monograph in several theoretical frameworks, including reciprocal empowerment, a values-driven model that focuses on power and suggests that changing the diversity climate is brought about through the collaboration of stakeholders at all levels. Without an examination of the power dynamics in institutions of higher education, change and progress will be slow to come. In contrast, the authors make clear the importance of understanding institutional dynamics, power, and context in advancing a diversity agenda. The monograph offers a theoretically based means to help institutional leaders who are seeking to breathe life into their vision statements and strategic plans. This monograph speaks to those in higher education who are left with the question of "how" once they have done all the elaborate assessments and visioning to determine "what."

One strength of this monograph is that it does not focus just on theory. Rather, it also provides concrete steps for institutions to follow in creating a genuinely inclusive campus. One of the most helpful sections of the monograph is on institutional self-assessment. It provides clear and distinct guidelines to move beyond a superficial review of an institution's position on different dimensions of diversity as a means to help stakeholders understand where they are with regard to diversifying their institution. Another very concrete section offers tactics to promote reciprocal empowerment on a campus. These ideas are rooted both in theory and research but also in daily practice and examples of institutions. This combination of theory, institutional examples, and hands-on suggestions for practice is particularly powerful and useful to readers.

Presidents, provosts, policymakers, researchers, governing boards, human resource and diversity practitioners, administrators, affirmative action officers, and faculty and staff committed to furthering their institutional progress on diversity will find this book a practical and valuable resource. Because the book focuses on results-oriented approaches, it will also be useful to diversity task forces and councils, multicultural centers, and other governance entities. I can see this book used as the basis for workshops or strategic planning groups as a way to figure out how to assess institutional diversity status and figure out ways to move a diversity agenda forward. It is a good book for graduate students and higher education scholars to use as an example of how to synthesize current literature and theory as a means to inform practice and improve institutional effectiveness.

Bridging the Diversity Divide is written to assist stakeholders at colleges and universities in continuing the discussion of why diversity is an important element needed to make research universities better. It offers steps institutions can take to make progress on their diversity agendas as they move from talk to action.

Lisa E. Wolf-Wendel
Series Editor

Acknowledgments

This monograph is dedicated to the next generation of leaders—Alexander David Chun, Shomari Evans, Jabari Evans, Kalil Evans, and Rashida VanLeer—to their courage, and to the promise this global millennium offers for their futures. We gratefully acknowledge the guidance of our editor, Lisa Wolf-Wendel, and her visionary commitment throughout the course of preparing this monograph. We especially wish to thank Professor Joe Feagin, Ella C. McFadden Professor in Sociology, Texas A&M University, for his continuous encouragement in the evolution of this project as well as his invaluable suggestions at various stages of the manuscript's development. We also thank Willis Walker, chief legal counsel and vice president for human resources, Kent State University, as well as Trustee Georgette Sosa Douglass and Trustee Levi Williams of Broward College for their unwavering support for diversity and inclusion in our institutional environments. We also thank Professor Maria Lima of the State University of New York at Geneseo and Professor Frank H. Wu of the University of Maryland and George Washington University for their helpful suggestions. Our anonymous reviewers provided us with important insights that helped us strengthen our focus. We would like to especially acknowledge the skilled research assistance of Kimberly Thompson.

Published online in Wiley InterScience
(www.interscience.wiley.com) • DOI: 10.1002/aehe.3501

The Changing Landscape and the Compelling Need for Diversity

A thousand years from now, anthropologists or their thirty-first-century successors will wonder. Poring over the recorded remains of what was the United States, they will search for reasons. "How," they will ask, "could so great a nation with so many advantages over its outside adversaries allow itself to be destroyed from within?"

[Bell, 1993, p. ix]

THE ELECTION OF BARACK OBAMA in 2008 as America's forty-fourth president and the first biracial president heralds a new era. As the editor of *The Nation* observed, this moment is "a milestone in America's scarred racial landscape and a victory for the forces of decency, diversity, and tolerance" (vanden Heuvel, 2008, para. 3). Despite the excitement of this important victory, the journey toward inclusion has barely begun. In fact, the myth persists that race has disappeared as a factor influencing the life outcomes of all Americans (Bonilla-Silva, 2006). Scholars indicate that we still live in a society in which racial considerations play a prominent role (Bonilla-Silva, 2006; Feagin, 2006). The social terrain, including most institutional spaces, is "significantly racialized," and powerlessness remains a "key feature of well-developed racial oppression" (Feagin, 2006, p. 47).

In light of the election, some would deny that discrimination still exists. A Washington Post–ABC News poll conducted just before President Obama's inauguration among a random sample of 1,079 adults, including 749 white respondents and 204 black, substantiates this view (Fletcher and Cohen,

2009). Only 26 percent of 1,079 respondents indicated that racism is a big problem, as opposed to 54 percent in a similar poll in 1996 (Fletcher and Cohen, 2009). Although 47 percent of the respondents thought blacks living in their community experience racial discrimination, 64 percent of the blacks responding indicated that it remains a problem (Fletcher and Cohen, 2009).

Since Reconstruction after the Civil War, only two black governors have been elected, and Barack Obama was only the third African American senator elected in U.S. history (Inniss, 2008). White women hold only eight of the nation's governorships and sixteen of its one hundred senatorial positions (Inniss, 2008). Of the top state appointments over the decade between 1997 to 2007, only 35 percent of the positions have been held by women and 16 percent by minorities ("Not Just a Glass Ceiling," 2008).

Similarly in higher education, women and minorities may appear to be represented in the professoriate and in administration, but change has been incremental and come slowly. For example, in four-year and two-year institutions combined, African American faculty hold 5.2 percent of all full-time faculty positions; in public research universities, only 3.6 percent of ladder-rank positions (U.S. Department of Education, 2005). The percentage of African American faculty holding full-time faculty positions has remained virtually unchanged for the last quarter century, ranging from only 4.2 percent in 1979 to 5.2 percent in 2005 (U.S. Department of Education, 2005). A recent study of 852 institutions of higher education reveals that the vast majority of men and women in senior administrative roles are white and that only 16 percent of senior administrators are from underrepresented groups (King and Gomez, 2008). As chief academic officer is the typical pathway to the presidency, it is particularly troubling that only 23 percent of the incumbents in senior academic roles are women and that fewer than 10 percent of chief academic officers are minorities (King and Gomez, 2008).

The powerful symbolism of this new American presidency must be accompanied by systematic and long-term change in American social institutions and in higher education. Such transformation will benefit from a cross-disciplinary approach that draws on the insights of the social sciences, humanities, and natural sciences to obtain unified understanding (Evans and Chun, 2007a). Bridging the diversity divide requires systemic change to overcome historical, behavioral, and organizational barriers to diversity and create inclusive campus environments. As practitioners in the higher education environment, we focus in this monograph on concrete approaches and tools that will assist educational leaders and educators in the creation of a genuinely inclusive campus culture.

One of the rallying calls of the Obama campaign in 2008 was "Respect, Empower, Include." The organizing principles of engagement, inclusion, and democratic participation epitomized the focus of the campaign. Similarly, in seeking to develop inclusive campus environments, we explore the model of reciprocal empowerment as a moral framework that links the institution's values, culture, and workplace practices to the outside world through the prism of diversity. Reciprocal empowerment comprises three powers: the power to define one's own identity (self-determination), the power to give oneself and others adequate resources (distributive justice), and the power to give oneself and others a voice (democratic participation) (Prilleltensky and Gonick, 1994).

In this exploration, we focus on public research universities to build on and operationalize the themes of an earlier monograph that examined diversity planning and behavioral and organizational barriers to diversity (Evans and Chun, 2007a). Public research universities have played a pioneering and instrumental role in twenty-first-century diversity strategic planning, probably as a result of requirements for public accountability, institutional size, and requirements to report compliance. These institutions rely to some degree on state funding and are required to maintain accountability to public constituents. Further, in the exploration of the impact of globalization on diversity, research universities provide a model for how individual differences can be transcended through communication and collaboration among diverse groups of scholars.

The sweeping forces of globalization have heightened the importance and priority of diversity in higher education. The word "diversity" broadly refers to characteristics that differentiate individuals such as gender, race, ethnicity, age, disability, sexual orientation, generational differences, and religious beliefs. These characteristics differentiate individuals from each other. A second meaning of diversity in higher education reflects a concern for inclusiveness and social justice or "the differences that differences make" (Owen, 2008, p. 187).

Because persistent barriers hinder the efforts of women and minorities to first gain entrance to and then remain in the sacred grove of academe (Cooper and Stevens, 2002), our use of the word "diversity" in this monograph is limited to discussion of the differences women and minority faculty and staff bring to campus environments. In the context of histories of exclusion, race and gender are especially salient and visible identities (Owen, 2008). In light of these past legacies, the goal of achieving a campus climate that supports racial and cultural diversity needs to be affirmed as a campus priority (Hurtado, Milem, Clayton-Pedersen, and Allen, 1999). Without explicitly addressing racial, ethnic, and gender diversity, universities will be unable to realize a true culture of diversity representative of the American and global landscape.

This chapter first provides an overview of forces that have historically inhibited the inclusion of women and minority faculty and staff in higher education. It then discusses how globalization has reshaped the landscape for higher education and created a compelling mandate for the attainment of inclusive campus environments. Next it examines the role of diversity as an intangible organizational capability linked to institutional excellence and quality. Finally, it introduces the frame of demography, diversity, and democracy that will embed reciprocal empowerment in the structures, culture, and practices of the university.

Constructing a Comparative Theoretical Framework

The debate generated during the 2008 Democratic presidential primaries over the notion of historical oppression and racism in America highlights the controversial nature of these topics. As a candidate for the presidency, Senator Barack Obama had to respond to considerable criticism regarding the rhetoric of his pastor, Reverend Jeremiah Wright. Reverend Wright's comments on widespread racism and governance by rich whites generated a firestorm of collective white indignation (Wise, 2008a). Reverend Wright termed America "the U.S. of K.K.A." (Kantor, 2008). In a pivotal speech on March 18, 2008, entitled "A More Perfect Union," Barack Obama renounced the incendiary remarks of his pastor but underscored the fact that "race is an issue . . . this nation cannot afford to ignore right now" (CBS News, 2008, p. 2).

This highly charged controversy regarding the existence and extent of racism in America clearly demonstrates a division of opinion on this issue. In this regard, a Washington Post–ABC News poll conducted in January 2009 reveals markedly different views on the impact of discrimination among whites and blacks (Fletcher and Cohen, 2009). Although 44 percent of black respondents indicated that racism still remains a big problem, only 22 percent of whites believe that it is (Fletcher and Cohen, 2009). Nearly three-quarters of blacks indicated that they had specifically experienced discrimination (Fletcher and Cohen, 2009).

Despite a relative lack of public recognition of the impact of discrimination, scholarly research directly links the existence of inequalities and forms of oppression to contemporary institutional and educational contexts (Bell, 1997; Cudd, 2006; Feagin, 2006; Feagin and Vera, 2001; Hardiman and Jackson, 1997; Hill Collins, 2000; Ropers-Huilman, 2008). As one scholar writes, the "fundamental injustice of social institutions" occurs when "institutionally structured harm" is directly or indirectly perpetuated on targeted groups through material and psychological forces that violate justice (Cudd, 2006, p. 26).

Privilege and oppression are two sides of the same coin, as they both limit modes of expression and choices (Ropers-Huilman, 2008). Systemic oppression of minority groups privileges whites (Yosso, Parker, Solorzano, and Lynn, 2004). White privilege represents an "invisible weightless knapsack" that from a structural perspective *systematically* confers unearned power (McIntosh, n.d.). Male privilege also takes place in systemic contexts and is another form of conferred dominance (McIntosh, n.d.).

Further, the phenomenon of oppression transpires when systemic and institutional discrimination are fused with personal bias, bigotry, and social prejudice (Bell, 1997). Oppressive power relations take place in the context of social relations that determine how groups are included or excluded from decision-making processes (Feagin and Vera, 2001). These relations also affect the development of identity, the sense of belonging, and individual dignity (Feagin and Vera, 2001). Forms of oppression take both active forms that we can see as well as embedded forms that members of dominant groups are taught not to see (McIntosh, n.d.). White privilege is "so woven into the unexamined institutional practices, habits of mind, and perceived truths that Americans can barely see it" (Brown and others, 2003, p. 4).

Critical race theory, a theory that first emerged in the 1970s among minority legal scholars that challenged how race and racial power are represented in American law, offers significant insights into how racism permeates social institutions and daily life. It contests the narrow, legal notion of racism as discrete and identifiable acts of prejudice and points to the ordinariness of racism in everyday social practices (Crenshaw, Gotanda, Peller, and Thomas, 1996; Delgado and Stefancic, 2001). Further, it illuminates how whiteness or the white identity contained in the law confers property rights on whites—the same privilege accorded to holders of other types of property (Harris, 1996).

Critical race theory also brings into question the control and production of knowledge by dominant groups and emphasizes the need to draw on the experiential knowledge of minorities (Bernal and Villalpando, 2002). Deeply embedded research epistemologies that emerge from the culture and social history of the dominant race have a negative impact on minorities as well as the scholarship they produce (Scheurich and Young, 1997). By identifying the epistemology of the dominant race as natural and appropriate, epistemological racism restricts and even delegitimizes different epistemologies arising from other racial cultures (Scheurich and Young, 1997). An "apartheid" of knowledge that marginalizes and devalues the scholarship of minority faculty still persists in higher education (Bernal and Villalpando, 2002).

Pervasive forms of social injustice are not only woven into institutional practices and norms but also can be internalized in the consciousness of those who are oppressed. Political oppression represents the creation of material barriers to the fulfillment of self-determination, distributive justice, and democratic participation, while psychological oppression takes place through the internalization of negative views of the self based on political domination (Prilleltensky and Gonick, 1996). As a result, the oppressed too can contribute to their own oppression through internalization and a process of "collusion" by which they accept their own devaluation (Hardiman and Jackson, 1997). This collusion can have a corrosive effect on the self-esteem of women and minorities (Evans and Chun, 2007a).

Multiple dimensions of oppression such as race, gender, class, and sexuality can intersect in institutions to create a complex matrix of domination (Hill Collins, 2000). These intersectional paradigms underscore the fact that oppressions work in concert to produce and heighten injustice (Hill Collins, 2000; McIntosh, n.d.). In higher education, these intersections for women faculty can take shape in a "dance of identities" in which both gender and race shape opportunities and experiences (Ropers-Huilman, 2008). Ironically, some liberal feminist perspectives have ignored the complexity of the intersection between sexism and racism (Darlington and Mulvaney, 2003). The omission of black feminist scholarship from the tradition of American feminist scholarly research has resulted in the suppression of black women's ideas and the further marginalization and isolation of black women, particularly in academic settings (Hill Collins, 2000; Moses, 1997).

Intersecting oppressions occur in three concurrent domains: (1) the *structural domain,* which reflects how social institutions are organized to maintain forms of exclusion over time; (2) the *disciplinary domain* in which organizational practices sustain existing power relations; and (3) the *interpersonal domain* of everyday interaction in which dominant ideology supplants the cultural ways of knowing of subordinated groups (Hill Collins, 2000). For example, Fred Bonner, an African American professor at a predominantly white institution, describes how the confluence of these dimensions creates a chilly climate at a micro level in departments and a macro level across the entire university (2006). Minority faculty members are caught in the continuous process of proving intellectual competence (structural domain); struggle to receive support for success in ongoing practices such as teaching, research, and service (disciplinary domain); and cope with a feeling of "otherness" in everyday interactions where they are often perceived as outsiders or house guests (interpersonal domain) (Bonner, 2006). In one of Bonner's multiple narratives entitled "I Have Everything to Prove," he writes, "I decided to move into faculty of color survival mode—plans for survival, in essence contingency plans, that faculty of color must have readily accessible to remain viable in the academy" (2006, p. 82).

From a historical perspective, predominantly white universities have a longer history of exclusion than they do of inclusion (Milem, Chang, and Antonio, 2005). Although in the United States public and private universities have been viewed as tolerant and open, in fact, they have often been the centers of racial exclusion (Feagin, Vera, and Imani, 1996). The legacy of racial discrimination remains entrenched in higher education in the United States (Feagin, Vera, and Imani, 1996). It persists in the psychosocial environment as well as the behavioral and organizational barriers that inhibit the progress of women and minorities. It persists in the prevalence of white racial framing—the integrated set of negative stereotypes, images, racialized emotions, assumptions, ideas, and patterns of behavior that have been learned and perpetuated in white social networks over generations (Feagin, 2006). It persists also in the existence of "social alexithymia"—an adaptation of the psychiatric phenomenon that describes individuals unable to understand or relate to the emotions and psychological pain of the targets of oppression (Feagin, 2006, p. 28).

The dominant group in power, which has generally comprised white males, through the course of time has imposed its cultural values on the organization through persistent influence (Kirton, 2003). This homogeneity creates pressure to conform coupled with a corresponding tendency to exclude those who do not "fit" the "dominant monoculture" (Kirton, 2003, p. 7). The pressure to conform is not limited simply to issues of race. When hegemonic gender beliefs become salient in an organization, these beliefs are accompanied by hierarchical assumptions about men's greater status and competence and differing traits and skills (Ridgeway and Correll, 2004).

Rather than demonizing individuals or labeling them "racist," the purpose of a structural understanding of racism is to uncover the practices that reinforce the contemporary racial order (Bonilla-Silva, 2003). The benefits of white privilege such as access to better career opportunities and psychological freedom from the burden of worrying about race cannot be underestimated (Wise, 2008b). Institutional practices have created "cumulative inequalities by race" in patterns of opportunity hoarding, while minorities have suffered from a corresponding disaccumulation of economic advantage (Brown and others, 2003, p. 22).

Through the actions of individuals in institutions, subtle forms of discrimination that arise from biases, prejudices, and stereotypes are reenacted, replayed, and performed. These socially generated actions replicate the normative structures, racial hierarchies, and inequalities embedded in these institutional settings (Feagin, 2006).

Like a mutant virus, discrimination has evolved into different forms more difficult to identify and combat (Gaertner and Dovidio, 2000). Subtle biases that permeate organizational behavior, thinking, and decision making are displayed in significantly different ways. Forms of "everyday discrimination" or covert discrimination have replaced direct and blatant acts of discrimination (Deitch and others, 2003; St. Jean and Feagin, 1998). Microaggressions and microincursions against minorities are cumulative, subtle, and repetitive. For example, a study of thirty-four African American students at three elite predominantly white research universities documents the "daily barrage of racial microaggressions" endured by these students both inside and outside their classes (Solorzano, Ceja, and Yosso, 2000, p. 70).

In fact, racial events—repetitive, recurring happenings in which racialized actions are performed, often in a ritualized manner—reflect the continued influence of centuries-old social exclusion (Picca and Feagin, 2007). A seemingly innocent example of a potentially racialized action is the way that minority professors may be called by their first names rather than "Doctor" or "Professor." Professor Tina Harris (2007) describes how the frequent omission of "Doctor" or "Professor" and its replacement with "Ms.," "Mrs.," or "Tina" by students addressing her in social and professional settings caused her to question why these interactions were occurring and appeared to communicate that she was unworthy of the respect afforded to her white male colleagues.

Given the persistence of institutional discrimination, what might be termed the "law of social inertia" will require a "major, unbalancing force" to counteract the exploitative social mechanisms of oppression (Feagin, 2006, p. 34). Globalization may indeed represent the unbalancing force that will overcome barriers to inclusion in the university. We now explore how globalization is altering the landscape for the research university and heightening the focus on talent.

Globalization and the New Landscape for Higher Education

The pressures of globalization represent a catalyst for change in higher education. The expansive power of globalization is rapidly diminishing national, economic, and cultural boundaries, transforming ways of sharing and developing knowledge, and reshaping the world as we know it. Like a tidal wave, globalization has altered irrevocably the features of how, where, when, and by whom work is performed. The world has indeed become a global village, just as the "American tapestry" has become increasingly diverse and multicultural (Firebaugh and Miller, 2000).

In this global context, universities bear significant responsibility for leadership, not only for the advancement of knowledge but also for the inclusiveness of the learning environment. As the pace of progress accelerates, institutions of higher education need more than ever to draw on the talents, knowledge, and abilities of diverse faculty and staff to compete in an economy in which the currency of knowledge is value (Brockbank, 1999; Kelly, 2006). Further, in its role as a leader in the quest for truth and knowledge, the university is the natural nexus for social change through its ability to foster dialogue, nurture free speech, and transcend boundaries (Barnett, 2005). The university can serve as a social compass—a place in which convergence and collaboration are the norm.

Higher education must now align and calibrate its educational programs and outcomes with the demands of a global society (Jones, 2005; Smith and Wolf-Wendel, 2005). Students need to be prepared for a workplace that requires broader cultural understanding and new skills (Jones, 2005). As institutions of higher learning prepare students for an era of explosive change, curricula, and literacies must also reflect the expanding frontier of knowledge.

Universities that have tried to enroll larger numbers of minority students recognize the contribution of diversity to the quality of the educational experience and have sought to enhance the prospects of minority students to contribute to mainstream America (Bowen, Bok, and Burkhart, 1999). Research indicates that socializing with individuals from different racial groups has a positive impact on the development of the individual white student (Chang, 1996, cited in Chang, n.d.). Similarly, the presence of diverse faculty role models broadens and enriches the educational experience of students. In this regard, a Ford Foundation survey of 2,011 voters in 1998 found widespread public support for the positive effect of diversity on the education of college students (Aguirre and Martinez, 2006).

The positive effects of emphasizing strong institutional diversity on student outcomes are documented in a study of 25,000 students at 217 institutions over four years (1985–1989) (Astin, 1993). The study found that emphasizing diversity tends to have uniformly positive effects, not only on educational outcomes but also on cultural awareness, student satisfaction, reduced materialism, and greater racial understanding (Astin, 1993).

From both practical and symbolic perspectives, a number of major developments have marked the advent of this new global era. We next discuss five areas that have reconfigured the world as we know it: the rise of new technologies, geopolitical shifts, the shrinking of barriers of time and distance, the growth in geographic centers of creativity and innovation, and the changing nature of employment.

First, a revolution in information communication technologies has fostered an age of democratized technology through the rise of the Internet, cellular phones, satellite communication, digitization, and miniaturization (Friedman, 1999). This historic change in the mode, manner, frequency, and ease of communication has triggered the proliferation of transnational corporations (Hansen and Salskov-Iversen, 2005).

Second, globalization has shifted the geopolitical balance of power. It has changed the world stage from one dominated by nation states to one in which roughly one hundred corporations, almost all headquartered in the United States, Europe, and Japan, dominate the world economy. Nation states that were once the central focus of power are being squeezed, on the one hand, by global economics and, on the other hand, by political efforts to devolve power (Stiglitz, 2006). The fall of the Berlin Wall on October 11, 1989, signaling the end of the Cold War was a watershed event that symbolized integration in the new global structure of economic and political power (Friedman, 1999). Globalization has increased individual freedom and revitalized cultures through the presence of foreign influences, markets, and technologies (Legrain, 2003). Ironically, the global wave of cultural change has in fact been driven by corporations (Visconti, 2007).

Third, from a metaphorical perspective, globalization is reconfiguring our perceptions of the shape and dimensions of the world (Florida, 2007; Friedman, 2005). These perceived changes have occurred through an evolutionary process that is progressively eroding the barriers of distance and difference. Globalization compresses both time and space in social relations (Florida, 2007; Mittelman, 1996). As Friedman (2005) indicates, the first era of globalization (1492 to 1800) shrank the world from size large to size medium as countries competed for resources through conquest, the second era (1800 to 2000) shrank the world from medium to small through corporations' competing for labor and markets, and the third era is shrinking the world to tiny. In fact, the current phase of globalization will be driven by a diverse group of individuals—non-Western and nonwhite (Friedman, 2005). And the current phase has also generated a new focus on talent, irrespective of the country, location, gender, or race of the individual contributor.

Different, but not necessarily competing, ways of describing this new universe have been proposed. The world can be seen as "flat" because it is a single global network in which convergence is the norm, knowledge centers are connected, and individuals collaborate across boundaries (Friedman, 1999). Or the world can be seen as "spiky," as economic productivity and innovation are highly concentrated in only a few regions and locations (Florida, 2007). This "spikiness" is vividly portrayed in maps of global activity that identify peaks and valleys of population density, patent statistics, energy use, and scientific advances (Florida, 2007). For example, Tokyo, Seoul, New York, and San Francisco lead in the number of patents; scientific advances are primarily concentrated in the United States and Europe; and certain large metropolitan areas continue to dominate in economic output (Florida, 2007).

Yet despite the appeal of metaphors suggesting changes in the contours of the earth, the underlying reality is that the fundamental curvature of the earth facilitates interconnection. The natural roundness of the world prevents us from falling off a flat surface into a black void, as the early explorers thought would occur if they ventured too far. Instead, the shape of the earth permits the confluence of communication and culture. Globalization now makes it imperative to build on these cultural interconnections both in our society and external to it in relation to the diverse societies that inhabit the world.

Fourth, the impact of sheer demographic dominance by nonwhite populations has changed the global equation. China, with its population of 1.3 billion, is already the second largest economy and expected to surpass the

United States as the largest economy in twenty years (Shenkar, 2006). China's advance is like that of the United States a century ago; it will represent the fundamental restructuring of the global business system (Shenkar, 2006). Half of India's 1.1 billion people are under age twenty-five, and its rapidly growing middle class is estimated to be as large as the entire population in the United States (Timmons, 2007). In the United States by no later than 2050, African American, Asian American, and Native American populations will be the new majority (Feagin, 2006). During the course of the next two generations, whites will become a statistical minority in most American cities, as they are already in half the nation's larger cities as well as in four states: Colorado, Texas, New Mexico, and Hawaii (Feagin, 2006).

In what has been described as the "post-American world," global transformation has occurred with the "rise of the rest" in the third great power shift of the modern era (Zakaria, 2008, p. 2). The rise of the western world in the fifteenth to eighteenth centuries was the first power shift, while the second shift occurred at the close of the nineteenth century with the rise of the United States (Zakaria, 2008). Without attention to the speed and impact of the forces of globalization, the United States and Western Europe could quickly fall behind. Other nations such as China and India have been able to jump-start processes of technological change without the burden of prior legacies or sunken costs in old systems (Friedman, 2005). Similarly, future American progress depends on our ability to discard past legacies and marshal the talents inherent in our demographically diverse society to overcome the historical divides of prejudice, exclusion, and the color line.

Although researchers clearly differ on the complex effect of globalization on white supremacy and the impact of the economic paradigm of neoliberalism with its emphasis on the free market and the control exercised by a handful of private interests (Ross and Gibson, 2007), our focus is on the compelling and urgent mandate that globalization presents for change in diversity in public research universities. Universities today seek to recruit diverse and talented faculty and staff faculty locally and abroad and collaborate across local, national, and international boundaries to extend the reaches of knowledge.

Fifth, globalization has dramatically altered the nature of jobs. Whereas employment security is no longer guaranteed, employability of the individual knowledge worker is now at the core of the new workforce reality (Kanter, 1991). Knowledge workers function virtually as independent entrepreneurs and need to remain current in terms of their marketable competencies in a global marketplace. The phenomenon of "dejobbing" describes the disappearance of jobs as social artifacts superimposed on the field of work to be done (Bridges, 1994). The old job paradigm that located employees at a certain level of a vertical and horizontal hierarchy has disappeared (Bridges, 1994). Workers are now responsible for their own career development across organizations and even across national boundaries (Bridges, 1994; Kanter, 1991).

Knowledge workers are highly mobile, carry with them their own means of production, work in nonlinear fashion, seek a match with their values in the workplace, know their jobs better than their supervisors, and seek work that will enhance their own capital of knowledge (Burud and Tumolo, 2004). Employers today have the challenge of creating meaningful jobs that will retain workers and ensure their continued motivation, innovation, and productivity. Jobs have the potential to either numb or stretch the mind, and just as individual IQ can be rated, so too can the learning quotient or IQ of a job be assessed (Kanter, 1991). Given the increased mobility of the workforce, employers cannot assume that workers will remain at a job without challenge or fulfillment.

While the nature of jobs is changing, the durability and useful life of current knowledge are also diminishing in some fields. Because the core work of the university pertains to the creation and transfer of knowledge, the talents and capabilities of faculty and staff drive the institution's ability to become a leader in intellectual innovation.

The Half Life of Knowledge

The increasingly rapid pace of change in today's global society has been accompanied by the swift obsolescence of knowledge. As a result, the useful life of knowledge is diminishing as its value and currency degrade more rapidly than ever before. Although this metaphor applies more aptly to certain disciplines than others, it nonetheless underscores how quickly knowledge can become outdated and irrelevant. At the same time, knowledge is rapidly expanding through scholarship and research.

From a theoretical perspective, the vastly increased speed of change is captured in what has been termed "the law of accelerating returns" (Kurzweil, 2005, p. 7). Inventor and futurist Ray Kurzweil builds on the theory of John von Neumann to indicate that the intuitive linear view of history has been replaced by a historical exponential view in which the rate of paradigm shift is now doubling every decade. In other words, progress is not a factor of adding a constant variable but of multiplying this constant variable, resulting in exponential change. Exponential growth starts out slowly and unnoticeably but suddenly becomes explosive and transformative (Kurzweil, 2005). As a result, the twenty-first century will encompass roughly the equivalent of twenty thousand years of progress—one thousand times greater than the twentieth century (Kurzweil, 2005).

The impact of globalization in eroding barriers of time and distance, creating new forms of communication, heightening the pace of progress, and creating a distinct focus on talent has transformed the university from "an institution that has always been circumscribed by time and geography to one without borders" (Atkinson, 2001, para. 1) The following sections explore how these changes ultimately affect the higher education enterprise. Specifically, they focus on the concept of intangible organizational capabilities that affect institutional success, arguing that diversity is an essential element in mobilizing the creative capital of the university to meet the challenges of globalization.

The Role of Intangibles in the Research University

As we explore further how globalization affects campus environments and workplace practices, emerging research in human resources provides valuable insights on the importance of developing organizational capabilities. This research indicates that when faced with the challenge of maintaining competitive advantage, "intangibles" are essential for organizational success (Ulrich and Smallwood, 2003). Intangibles are factors such as talent, shared mind-set, speed, innovation, efficiency, and collaboration and have been shown to influence financial outcomes and the bottom line (Ulrich, 1998a; Ulrich and Smallwood, 2003). For example, a study of 3,000 corporate firms over a decade indicates a positive relationship between a high-performance human resource system that capitalizes on intangible organizational capabilities and financial results (Ulrich and Creelman, 2006; Ulrich and Smallwood, 2004).

Following this line of reasoning, diversity is also a decisive and differentiating intangible in the higher education environment that is integral to institutional excellence and quality. Leveraging diversity provides a powerful source of competitive advantage by positioning the university to maintain synergy and congruence with a diverse global society. Because the pressure to change institutional culture is now coming from the outside in, strategically proactive strategies that maximize cultural characteristics will in turn optimize such an advantage (Brockbank, 1999).

From the standpoint of resources, faculty and staff represent the institution's intellectual and creative capital, the talent that drives the engine of academe. Creative capital is in fact an organization's most significant asset (Florida and Goodnight, 2005). One major American corporation acknowledges that 95 percent of its assets drive through the gates each night and return each morning (Florida and Goodnight, 2005). Such capital is the institution's only appreciable asset, as other assets such as equipment and facilities depreciate immediately (Ulrich, 1998a).

Creative or intellectual capital is built on the equation of competence times commitment: employee competence is multiplied by the value of employee commitment or the discretionary energy that employees give voluntarily through their involvement (Ulrich, 1998a; Ulrich and Smallwood, 2003). Yet an enhanced equation is needed to capture the intensity and impact of globalization on higher education today. In this expanded equation, employee commitment and competence have a third multiplier—the factor of diversity. As a multiplier, diversity has the capability of unleashing and mobilizing an institution's full talent potential. These factors provide the intellectual and creative capabilities needed to advance knowledge, sustain innovation, and keep pace with the doubling paradigm shift that occurs each decade.

Despite the frequent presupposition that diversity implies a compromise in quality, the concept of "inclusive excellence" recognizes that diversity and quality combine to form an alloy that is different from its constituent elements—both stronger and more durable (Clayton-Pedersen and Musil,

2005). If the perceived conflict between diversity and quality is not addressed, the challenge of diversity will not be met (Smith and Wolf-Wendel, 2005). Institutions need to broaden their understanding of quality and overcome the tendency to perpetuate homogeneity in the name of quality (Smith and Wolf-Wendel, 2005). Instead, diversity must be understood as a factor that enhances rather than diminishes quality and creates a richer, more vibrant whole.

Florida (2007) describes the needed fuel to propel progress toward economic development in a global society as comprised of three elements: technology, talent, and tolerance. From the perspective of diversity, his research suggests that tolerance is a critical component in a geographic region's or country's ability to mobilize creative talent (Florida, 2007). This research confirms the hypothesis that talent is attracted to regions where diversity and tolerance are greater and entry barriers lower for human capital (Florida, 2002a; Lee, Florida, and Acs, 2004). For example, one study examined the percentage of population with a bachelor's degree, percentage of professional and technical workers, and percentage of scientists and engineers and linked the percentages to the diversity index that measured the proportion of coupled gay households in a region's population (Florida, 2002a). The results of another study support the argument that creativity and diversity in a region generate more entrepreneurial activity and are more fundamental resources for entrepreneurship than tax rate, human or venture capital, or entrepreneurial zone (Lee, Florida, and Acs, 2004).

Transposing this argument to higher education institutions shows several interesting and significant parallels. Just as talented individuals are drawn to open and diverse regions, talented and diverse faculty and staff also seek environments where they can thrive. They will make informed choices in terms of working for institutions that are tolerant and open to diversity. Conversely, they will avoid environments that make it clear success is not possible.

Great universities with star faculty and outstanding research departments serve as magnets to attract talent and draw outside companies, laboratories, and venture capitalists to nearby locations (Florida, 2006). Yet when an institution of higher education fails to draw on the talent and creative capital of diverse faculty and staff, this capital is irrevocably wasted, squandered, and lost.

The failure to draw on this capital leads to the phenomenon of the revolving door and an endless, cyclical talent search (Thomas, 1990). In this regard, a study of one hundred elite white males in positions of power and authority found that many do not recognize African Americans as equals or as individuals much like themselves (Feagin and O'Brien, 2003). Misrecognition or the failure to recognize others leads to a tremendous loss of talent and reproduces historic institutional patterns of exclusion, privilege, and inequality (Feagin and O'Brien, 2003).

The toll arising from wasting talent is twofold. It affects not only the persons involved but also the institutions they serve. As Feagin (forthcoming) points out, "When people of color and white women are oppressed or marginalized in our major institutions not only do they suffer personally and in their communities, but also the institutions of which they are part suffer heavily, and eventually will deteriorate and decline. Excluding and marginalizing people of color and white women, who make up two-thirds of the people in a society like the US, means excluding the great amount of human knowledge, creativity, and deep understandings that they hold in their individual heads and collective memories. No society can last that ignores this great store of knowledge." The framework of talent, technology, and tolerance requires amplification as universities seek to maximize their talent potential and respond to the urgent pressures and opportunities of globalization.

The Frame of Demography, Diversity, and Democracy

An expanded model for attracting and retaining creative capital in higher education moves beyond the notion of mere tolerance for diversity to a framework based on respect, recognition and genuine inclusion. As scholars and practitioners have noted, a culture of respect provides a foundation for other elements that enhance the academic and administrative workplace (Brase, 2005; Gappa, Austin, and Trice, 2007). For example, the University of California, Irvine model for sustaining administrative improvement recognizes that the principal role of management is "to excel in the behaviors that lead to workplace respect—the foundation on which desired organizational patterns and, ultimately, performance critically depend" (Brase, n.d., p. 40). Conversely, a lack of respect causes faculty and staff members to feel not valued, to be disenfranchised from their institution's work, and to experience low levels of motivation (Gappa, Austin, and Trice, 2007). The absence of a culture of respect intensifies the isolation and alienation of minority and female faculty and staff and ultimately affects performance. As one faculty member observes, "In addition to the pain of working hard and being harshly evaluated, a feeling of unfairness makes the experiences of female faculty of color difficult" (Muhtaseb, 2007, p. 32).

A broader and more inclusive model is needed, one that encompasses the pluralistic context of American society, its core values, and the new global topography. To amplify the model of talent, technology, and tolerance, we suggest a framework that addresses the trilogy of demography, diversity, and democracy in our campus environments (Prewitt, 2002). This multidimensional frame overcomes the narrowness of mere tolerance and, through the synergy of these three elements, paves the way to genuine inclusion.

Demography provides an important opportunity for purposeful innovation— an advantage that it would be "sheer folly" to ignore (Drucker, 1985, p. 134). As institutions approach a diverse future, those that handle diversity strategically and are willing to share power will thrive, as opposed to institutions that hoard power and ironically endanger the very enterprise itself (Robbins, 2007).

The powerful impact of changing demography in the United States is captured in the new racial census categories of Census 2000—a late, but long needed acknowledgment of the complex, rich racial heritage of this country. Multiracial categories now replace the singular racial classifications of the past two centuries. This blended conception of diversity creates an unstable racial taxonomy that upsets traditional notions of race and emphasizes the multiplicity of our origins (Prewitt, 2002). The variety and complexity of American demography is captured in this more accurate reflection of the racial and ethnic blending present in the current population.

Student demography at public research universities has clearly shifted over the past decade with the increasing representation of minority students (Table 1). The dramatic increase in student demographic diversity provides a compelling rationale for devoting institutional attention and resources to the

TABLE 1

Change in Enrollment by Race at Public Research Universities, Fall 1994 to Fall 2004

	2004	1994	Numerical Change	Percent Change
Total Nonresident Aliens	207,610	153,686	53,924	35%
Total Black Non-Hispanic	307,360	209,905	97,455	46%
Total American Indian/Alaska Native	29,074	21,701	7,373	34%
Total Asian or Pacific Islander	263,226	187,906	75,320	40%
Total Hispanic	227,965	143,122	84,843	59%
Total White Non-Hispanic	2,430,507	2,298,968	131,539	6%
Total Race/Ethnicity Unknown	167,466	73,058	94,408	129%

Source: U.S. Department of Education, 2007.

attainment of greater representation of women and minorities among faculty and staff. Later in the chapter, we discuss the Supreme Court's recognition of the value of diversity in the educational process.

As research universities seek to address the demographic underrepresentation of faculty and staff, a danger may exist when the use of international talent to satisfy the university's diversity requirements is disproportionately emphasized. The predominant emphasis on international talent in some studies (see, for example, Florida, 2007) can inadvertently divert attention from the pressing need to address America's own demographic and sociohistorical realities. We would argue that universities are already uniquely positioned to address the ethnic and racial diversity of America today. This existing demographic diversity has not been tapped proportionately or sufficiently in terms of hiring patterns in higher education (Evans and Chun, 2007a). Although attracting international talent is one aspect of a recruitment program, a comprehensive talent strategy must aggressively address the underrepresentation of American women and minorities in faculty and staff ranks. New efforts toward inclusion that simply focus on international scholars and world cultures obscure the domestic issues that have led to affirmative action and do little for American minorities (Tapia, 2007).

In light of the importance of the multidimensional framework of demography, diversity, and democracy, we now turn to the pivotal concept of reciprocal empowerment. Reciprocal empowerment provides a vehicle that can localize this framework in institutional culture, practices, and processes. It is a mode of interaction that will counteract, neutralize, and progressively overcome regressive and resistant patterns of discrimination that still persist in the higher education workplace.

Reciprocal Empowerment Revisited

The reciprocity involved in empowerment is a critical dimension in personal and institutional transformation. As a core ideology, reciprocal empowerment can foster the transformational change needed to attain true diversity and is an essential element in an organizational identity that transcends periodic environmental shifts (Anderson, 2007). It is the antithesis of oppression and asymmetric power relations that limit self-determination, perpetuate social injustice, and suppress the participation and voice of vulnerable persons (Prilleltensky and Gonick, 1996). Further, reciprocal empowerment fosters democratic participation. This section presents specific examples of how this values-based approach based on self-determination, distributive justice, and collaboration will help foster a culture of inclusion.

What is the meaning of self-determination in academe? According to a minority female faculty member, it is the ability to determine "who we are, rather than having our identities designated by others" (Gonzalez, 1995, p. 88). She notes that minorities have frequently brought the influence of outside stereotyping into these definitions, including "an emphasis on our shortcomings, our sufferings, our obstacles, to the exclusion of our strengths and achievements. A culture with dignity sees its potential with as much clarity as it sees its history of oppression" (Gonzalez, 1995, p. 88). Another professor writes of the fact that her difference is "equated with inferiority" (Cruz, 1995, p. 93). She adds, "One of the painful results of feeling inferior was that I was compelled to revise my identity. (Truthfully, there were times when I wished I could slip out of who I am)" (p. 93).

Distributive justice refers to the reallocation of resources and opportunities stemming from the systematic deprivation of such resources by dominant forces in society (Prilleltensky and Gonick, 1994). For example, African

American administrators in predominantly white institutions in one study indicated that lack of supervisory support in some cases caused them to be ineffective in their positions through budgetary constraints, exclusion from meetings or initiatives, and denial of programming (Patitu and Hinton, 2003). This restriction of opportunity furthered the marginalization of these administrators and restricted their contributions to the institution.

The third pillar of reciprocal empowerment—collaboration and democratic participation—references partnership and participation in decision making (Prilleltensky and Gonick, 1994). When women or minorities holding positions of presumed authority lack decision-making authority, this absence is a clear signal of their token status. In this regard, tokenism can be seen as the incorporation of mannequins into university culture—persons hired for show, with arms and legs arranged so as to depict a certain pose and used to appease racial and ethnic communities, but with weak authority (Valverde, 2003).

Reciprocal empowerment enriches those who share power as well as those who become empowered. When those in power work to eliminate injustice and asymmetric power relations, they in turn liberate themselves from the perpetuation of privilege and oppression. The reciprocity in empowerment promotes conscientization or the critical consciousness that leads to a search for self-affirmation (Freire, 1989). Conscientization is a process that illuminates awareness of the psychological, cultural, and political conditions that determine the reality of individuals and of groups as well as the capacity to transform it (Prilleltensky and Gonick, 1996).

In the context of higher education, a study of thirty-eight African American women in educational administration illustrates reciprocal empowerment by demonstrating the power of sponsorship in fostering career success among minority women (Allen, Jacobson, and Lomotey, 1995). Sponsors in this study provided access to professional organizations, recommended individuals for senior positions, and shared privileged information (Allen, Jacobson, and Lomotey, 1995). As one respondent who was sponsored by an influential university professor indicates, "When I tell people who my sponsor is, they pay attention. I would never have been able to succeed as I have without his help" (Allen, Jacobson, and Lomotey, 1995, p. 418). Moreover, the potential mutuality of contributions occurs when individuals receive leadership support and are engaged as partners (D. A. Thomas, 2006).

Reciprocal empowerment provides a basis for understanding the ways in which the research university's culture, climate, practices, policies, and norms promote or inhibit the meaningful participation of women and minorities in institutional life and decision making. It opens the door to the enrichment and infusion of talent that drives institutional excellence and quality.

For comparative purposes, we contrast the framework of reciprocal empowerment that values the diversity of women and minority faculty and staff with the framework of systemic racism (Feagin, 2006). Figure 1 depicts how the self-perpetuating racial hierarchy of domination can take shape in institutional contexts (Feagin, 2006). In contrast, the model of reciprocal empowerment shown in Figure 2 draws on the multidimensional framework of demography, diversity, and democracy to transform these dimensions and fundamentally alter institutional topology.

FIGURE 1
Systemic Racism

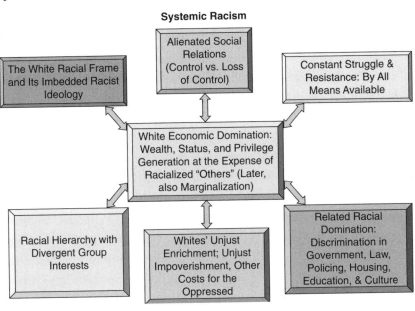

Source: Feagin, 2006, p. 17.

FIGURE 2
Framework of Reciprocal Empowerment

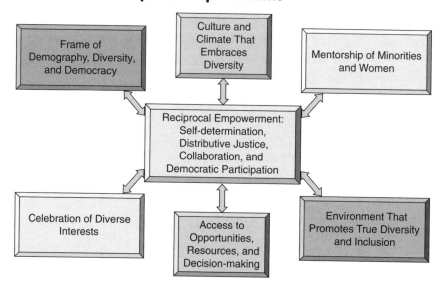

As the comparison between these two frameworks suggests, culture change in higher education demands sustained organizational attention to deeply embedded, socially derived barriers to diversity.

The concept of psychological empowerment is closely allied with reciprocal empowerment and helps to clarify how the individual's sense of fulfillment and efficacy can be enhanced. According to Thomas and Velthouse (1990), empowerment is reflected in four cognitions reflecting an individual's relationship to specific tasks in his or her work role: *meaning* (fit between work role and individual values); *competence* (belief in one's ability to perform work activities); *choice or self-determination* (sense of choice in determining work actions); and *impact* (degree to which an individual can affect strategic or operational outcomes) (Spreitzer, 1995, 1996; Thomas and Velthouse, 1990).

Building on this theory, Spreitzer (1995) proposes a multidimensional measure of empowerment validated through research in two organizations. The model, shown in Figure 3, identifies four positive antecedents to psychological empowerment: *locus of control,* in which individuals exercise some control over their work environment; *self-esteem,* which occurs when individuals

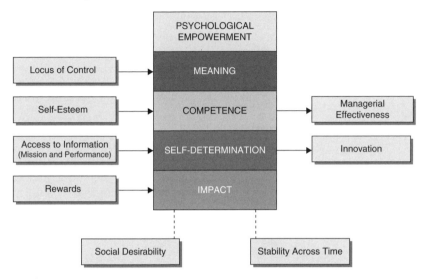

Source: Spreitzer,1995.

view themselves as valued and talented contributors; *access* to valuable institutional information; and the potential of *rewards* for performance (Spreitzer, 1995).

Clearly, psychological empowerment is congruent with key characteristics of reciprocal empowerment, although its primary focus is on individual motivation and cognition. Self-esteem enhances self-determination, access to information exemplifies distributive justice, and potential for rewards and locus of control are markers of meaningful participation in organizational life.

From an institutionwide perspective, empowering workplaces provide opportunities rather than constraints on employee participation (Spreitzer, 1996). Such environments promote high levels of involvement and commitment, heighten trust, and enhance employees' influence in decision making (Spreitzer, 1996). Empowered individuals in turn exert reciprocal influence by fostering empowerment in their work environments, although the work environment tends to have more impact on individuals than the converse (Spreitzer, 1996).

One of the most significant research findings in this regard links psychological empowerment with the facilitation of innovation (Spreitzer, de Janasz, and Quinn, 1999). A study of 393 midlevel supervisors from a Fortune 500 organization found that supervisors who felt empowered exhibited change-oriented leadership behavior and were viewed by their subordinates as more innovative, inspiring, and upward influencing (Spreitzer, de Janasz, and Quinn, 1999).

In summary, reciprocal empowerment provides a new vista of opportunity for realizing the power of the "intangible" of diversity in the quest for institutional excellence. To counteract the corrosive forces of racial and gender inequality that persist in higher education, reciprocal empowerment forms a bridge across the diversity divide to the American tradition of opportunity— the opportunity for each person to succeed and have a stake in our society (Atkinson and Pelfrey, 2006). Although affirmative action has often created a backlash of public sentiment, opportunity is something every American can understand (Atkinson and Pelfrey, 2006). In this sense, reciprocal empowerment embodies opportunity, collaboration, and participation. By revisiting the concept of reciprocal empowerment in this book, we seek to present specific approaches that will assist institutions of higher education in the effort to attain greater inclusion for women and minority faculty and staff.

Guided by a theoretical framework that recognizes the impact of sociohistorical forces of exclusion, in this chapter we have seen how the external forces of globalization create pressure for internal change in the university. These countervailing pressures have the potential to unseat and unbalance long-standing institutional barriers to inclusion. We have proposed a frame of demography, diversity, and democracy as the vehicle for such evolutionary change and described how reciprocal empowerment can transform the university landscape in the quest for inclusion.

Translating Principles into Practice

> Our country's enormous racial and ethnic diversity—drawn from all corners of the globe—is a potential source of great strength. And that strength from diversity is essential to thriving in today's complex world. But to realize that strength depends on our ability to use and appreciate that diversity. To recognize it as an indispensable democratic value. It requires us to know ourselves. To have confidence in ourselves.
>
> [Payton, 2005, para. 32]

JOHN PAYTON, LEAD COUNSEL for the University of Michigan in *Gratz* v. *Bollinger* [539 U.S. 244 (2003)], eloquently describes the role of diversity as an American strength and democratic value that requires us to know ourselves and have confidence in who we are. The goal of reciprocal empowerment similarly challenges educational leaders to translate principles into practice and actualize the unique strength that derives from demography, diversity, and democracy.

What are the initial points of consideration for the university in terms of addressing the larger trends of globalization in its workforce? How do these focal points promote the transformation of institutional culture? We suggest three areas of consideration that link the purposes of the university with diversity and globalization: institutional mission, the educational process, and talent management.

Globalization and Institutional Mission

The starting point for framing the vision of diversity in the research university is institutional mission. Institutional mission crystallizes what an institution strives to accomplish, for it defines purpose and values. It communicates strategic intent and energizes the institution through its "stretch" goals (Hamel and Prahalad, 1989). Arguably, this mission needs to consider the changing demographics of student populations, the increased demands of a global society in the educational process, and the institution's intended responsiveness to these changing realities.

University leadership has become increasingly aware of both the promise and the challenges that globalization represents in defining the university's role. For example, upon accepting his appointment as the president of Indiana University, Michael McRobbie highlighted the broad global reach of the research university: "Our message must travel from Bloomington to Bangalore, from South Bend to Shanghai. We must compete for, and be accessible to, the best faculty and students in the world, regardless of their race, gender, religion, or nationality. Our vision must be both local and global. We must serve the State while focusing on the international horizon" (McRobbie, 2007, paras. 2–4). President McRobbie's message articulates the role of the research university in seeking talent, regardless of race, gender, national origin, or religion, and in transcending differences in the search for talented faculty and students.

Institutional mission and vision statements represent the most visible strategic opportunity to articulate a commitment to diversity. Yet, surprisingly, a review of 312 institutional mission statements for institutions listed in *The Princeton Review* found that only 11.2 percent referenced becoming knowledgeable about diversity as a goal, while 21.5 percent included appreciating diversity. A larger percentage (41.3 percent) included student diversity in their mission statements (Meacham and Barrett, 2003).

Similarly among public research universities, examples of mission statements that relate the values of diversity and empowerment to faculty and staff inclusion are difficult to find. An alternative and more prevalent model has been to identify diversity as an institutional value. Another prominent vehicle for articulating diversity mission is the creation of a diversity vision statement. Practices at the following universities exemplify the different mission statements:

The University of Connecticut, Storrs. The central mission statement of the University of Connecticut indicates that "through research, teaching, service, and outreach, we embrace diversity and cultivate leadership, integrity, and engaged citizenship in our students, faculty, staff, and alumni" (Board of Trustees, 2006, para. 1).

Indiana University, Bloomington. The mission statement of Indiana University at Bloomington links diversity to the work environment by stating that "Indiana University strives to achieve full diversity, and to maintain friendly, collegial, and humane environments, with a strong commitment to academic freedom" (Indiana University, 2005, para. 1).

The University of California at Irvine. A lengthier statement on diversity is included as part of the university's strategic plan; it addresses the obligation to increase participation among racial, ethnic, and cultural groups that are underrepresented among faculty, students, and staff (University of California, Irvine, 2007).

Kent State University, Kent, Ohio. The university's diversity vision is linked to the institution's mission statement in the strategic diversity plan. The vision statement emphasizes the university's commitment to build an environment that is "welcoming, affirming and empowering to all people" and promotes participation in a diverse, democratic global society (Kent State University, n.d.).

Recognition of the Value of Diversity in the Educational Process

One of the principal arguments for diversity that has evolved through legal challenges is its value in the educational process. In the recent debate about affirmative action in admissions policies, the Supreme Court readdressed and reaffirmed the value of diversity on college and university campuses. Building on the affirmation of the value of diversity in the educational progress articulated in *Regents of the University of California* v. *Bakke* [438 U.S. 265 (1978)], the 2003 Supreme Court decisions relating to admissions at the University of Michigan (*Grutter* v. *Bollinger,* 539 U.S. 306 and *Gratz* v. *Bollinger*) upheld the importance of diversity as a compelling state interest. These decisions, however, like *Bakke,* continue to insist on a narrowly tailored definition of how race can be used in the admissions process based on a process of strict scrutiny. Most significant perhaps, these decisions reversed the rulings of the Fifth Circuit in Texas, Louisiana, and Mississippi that made it unlawful to consider race in the admissions process (Valentine, 2003). As a result of specific state referenda, however, California and Washington have determined that race cannot be used in admissions, while Florida made a similar determination for public universities through governmental executive order (Valentine, 2003).

Although focused on admissions practices, the University of Michigan decisions form an interpretive legal benchmark that underscores the importance of diversity in the educational experience. Yet some scholars argue that despite this support for diversity in the *Bakke* and *Grutter* decisions, these cases narrowed the arguments for affirmative action in admissions by emphasizing tolerance for social differences to the virtual exclusion of efforts to remedy social discrimination and implicit racism (Ford, 2005; Harris, 1999). Ford (2005) observes, "In this light it would appear that a central function of 'diversity' is to finesse, if not obscure, the salience of contemporary racism" (p. 36). For this reason, the diversity rationale introduced in *Bakke* and *Grutter* becomes dangerous when it enshrines diversity as the sole or primary reason race is significant (Ford, 2005). In ignoring the effects of systemic discrimination, the decision unwittingly laid the groundwork for arguments about "reverse discrimination," "preferential treatment," and "unfairness to whites" (Harris, 1999, p. 134). Even if unintentionally, the decision fosters a focus on the benefits to educational institutions rather than the unfair obstacles confronting minority students (Harris, 1999).

From a historic perspective, the Michigan cases represent the evolution of a legal tradition that has its roots in the historic *Brown v. Board of Education* [347 U.S. 483 (1954)]. The *Brown* decision came at a time of great racial inequality in the United States; it was a landmark effort by the Court to insist that legalized racial inequality should not continue by dismantling the apparatus of segregation in the public schools (Ogletree, 2004). The Court weakened the force of its decisions by allowing proponents of segregation to delay the end of segregation under the rubric of accomplishing this end with "all deliberate speed" (Ogletree, 2004). Nonetheless, the *Brown* decision challenged society to acknowledge the value of tolerance, respect, equality, and social justice that emanates from an inclusive community. It underscored the role of diversity in American democracy. Rather than pointing backward to historic trends of exclusion, the *Brown* decision seemed to point toward significant efforts to debalkanize public education.

Yet a half century after *Brown,* the "slow, circuitous climb" to justice has been followed by a rapid retreat through a series of decisions by the Supreme Court from 1974 to the present (Pettigrew, 2004, p. 521). This decline began with the decision in *Milliken* v. *Bradley* [418 U.S. 717 (1974)] that struck down a district court's efforts to overcome segregation in Detroit public schools (Pettigrew, 2004). In 2007, this regressive trend culminated in the conservative Court's dramatic five to four ruling overturning school desegregation plans in Seattle, Washington, and Louisville, Kentucky, that used race as a factor in determining where students attend classes. The post-*Bakke* university essentially ignores the discrimination suffered by applicants in schools and evades a rigorous assessment of the effects of racism and bigotry in favor of a discussion about culture (Ford, 2005). The Berlin walls that came down in 1989 in favor of a united Germany have only grown stronger in America (Pettigrew, 2004). The Court's recent reactionary decisions challenge American educational institutions to become more democratic and more inclusive in the noble tradition of *Brown.*

Talent Management

Given the importance of creative capital in building competitive advantage, talent management has now become an institutional imperative. Typically more than three-quarters of a university's resources are expended in personnel costs. Although in the past higher education has not had to deal head on with market forces, the reality of leaner workforces and shrinking budgets demands that institutions of higher education manage more effectively with fewer resources. In light of these trends, strategic workforce planning must provide the ability to recruit and retain a diverse workforce in addressing the institution's talent needs.

As a result, we propose six guiding principles focused on talent management to help navigate the currents of globalization, diminishing resources, and heightened competition. In an era of accelerated change with rapidly diminishing boundaries of time and space, early recognition of the value and contributions of diversity and inclusion provides a channel to sustaining and enhancing intellectual advancement, creativity, and innovation among faculty and staff.

Principle 1. A Comprehensive Approach to Talent Management Facilitates the Attainment of Diversity

A comprehensive talent strategy will lead to the attainment of diversity through the recruitment and retention of diverse and talented faculty and staff. "Talent management" refers to institutional practices designed to attract, retain, and develop the workforce and is recognized as the principal driver of organizational success (Lockwood, 2006). This guideline presumes that campus recruitment and hiring policies require diverse search committees, search committee training, broad advertising, approaches that consider nontraditional candidates, and other practices that promote consideration of diverse talent. Without these structural safeguards, search processes can become unfocused and even exclusionary.

Contrary to the presumption that diversity and quality are separate, an initiative undertaken by the Association of American Colleges and Universities (Making Excellence Inclusive) is designed to help institutions of higher education integrate diversity and educational quality and to embed these efforts in the academic and institutional mission (Association of American Colleges and Universities, 2009).

The emphasis on talent management needs also to be considered in relation to what have been termed "A Positions"—positions that have disproportionate importance in relation to the ability to execute organizational strategy and in which a wide variability in the quality of work can be exhibited by employees in the position (Huselid, Beatty, and Becker, 2005). These positions have a greater impact on institutional strategy and performance and require a greater investment in talent (Huselid, Beatty, and Becker, 2005). A five-year study of major companies that went from good to great as measured by a substantial cumulative increase in stock returns reveals that having the right people in the right seats is an important differentiating factor (Collins, 2001).

In higher education, such key positions have the potential to further institutional goals and to nurture and advance creativity and innovation. The magnet talent represented by leading professors in certain disciplines that differentiate a university's offerings and strengths illustrates the impact of what could be considered "A Positions." For example, the University of Pennsylvania rose from sixteenth in the *U.S. News & World Report* rankings in 1994 to sixth in 2006 using a strategy that included recruitment and retention of an even more eminent faculty (Farrell and Van Der Werf, 2007). The premise that a comprehensive talent strategy facilitates the attainment of diversity recognizes the importance of creativity, innovation, and intelligence in fulfilling the purposes of the university and how these dimensions transcend differences in race, ethnic origin, gender, age, disability, sexual orientation, or other factors. Diverse talent enriches an institution's ability to further its mission and goals and create a legacy of inclusion.

Principle 2. Diverse Talent Brings Knowledge and Intelligence to the Institution

Diverse talent is a source of great knowledge, intelligence, creativity, and innovation. When diverse faculty and staff are excluded, the collective ignorance level increases. Conversely, when women and minority faculty and staff are empowered, institutional knowledge, know-how, and creativity increase exponentially.

As discussed earlier in the chapter, invention, knowledge, and creativity are the backbone of the university in maintaining competitive advantage. For this reason, sustaining relative competitive advantage depends on accelerating organizational learning to create new advantages rather than imitating competitors or simply emulating past practices (Hamel and Prahalad, 1989). The "spikiness" that derives from the convergence of talent, creativity, and innovation (Florida, 2007) requires active cultivation to build the critical mass of diverse talent needed for creative achievement. Because an atmosphere of tolerance is linked to the development of such "spikiness," a culture of reciprocal empowerment nurtures creative development. No society can survive based on the knowledge of the statistical minority, not the 37 percent who are white male in the United States, or even the knowledge of white males who hold 45.4 percent of administrator positions and 55.1 percent of full-time tenure-track or tenured faculty positions in public doctoral research universities (U.S. Department of Education, 2005).

Principle 3. Recruitment and Retention of Talented and Diverse Faculty and Staff Is Continuous

Even when specific vacancies do not exist, the need to identify potential talent continues. To create diverse pools of talent, recruitment efforts need to access not only individuals who are seeking positions but also those who are successful in their current institutions. Recruitment is an ongoing, active, and aggressive process of garnering the necessary talent for the university's strategic and ever-changing workforce.

Perhaps less recognized is the fact that retention is also continuous. The marginalization of talent, whether accidental, unconscious, or reflective of cultural patterns in an institution, eventually results in the attrition of valuable assets. Little attention is often given to this loss of talent; instead, individual histories of isolation or even institutional mistreatment are frequently viewed as anomalies (Evans and Chun, 2007a).

Creative individuals aspire to work in environments and organizations that value their contributions and input, challenge them, have mechanisms to mobilize resources in support of ideas, and are responsive to both small innovations and the occasional very significant idea (Florida, 2002b). Retention of these individuals requires not only some degree of continuity and stability but also an atmosphere of diversity and broad-mindedness that permits creativity to flourish (Florida, 2002b).

Principle 4. The Focus on Talent Is Prospective Rather Than Retrospective and Models the Values of Democracy in a Global Society

Rather than a backward-looking focus on remedying underrepresentation through affirmative action, the focus on talent is forward looking and seeks to model the society of the present and future in its workforce. As a result, the focus on diverse talent is not reactive, but proactive. It represents a commitment to the values of a democratic society through the empowerment of a diverse community of scholars and administrators.

Principle 5. Organizational Compassion Is a Key Twenty-First-Century Approach That Enhances Institutional Awareness and Sensitivity

Institutions that support and enact reciprocal empowerment are compassionate organizations. They engage in collective noticing, collective feelings of concern for others, and collective responding to pain in the organization (Kanov and others, 2006). The recognition of the importance of a compassionate organization builds on the notion of interconnection, collective mindfulness, and a collective memory system that is engaged and aware (Kanov and others, 2006). A compassionate organization is one that exhibits understanding and concern for the needs of its workforce. It recognizes the signals of marginalization and exclusion and works to correct them.

Principle 6. A Strategic Approach to Talent Management Necessarily Encompasses Attention to the Future Evolution of Workplace Culture to Be Welcoming, Inclusive, and Reflective of Demographic Diversity

As a workplace intangible, attainment of a critical mass of diverse individuals is a stepping stone toward the attainment of a workplace supportive of diversity. In the process of transformation, institutional leadership with the assistance of human resource professionals and other key offices and campus constituencies can help guide the progress toward a more inclusive workplace.

Whereas labels and stereotypes have been used to separate people, globalization enables individuals to write their own labels, burst out of categorizing boxes, and engage the world in terms of their strengths, talents, and abilities (Graham, 2006). University leadership can assist with this process by supporting the divestiture of traditional labels, stereotypes, and behavioral barriers.

Concluding Observations

The paradigm shifts outlined in this chapter that accompany the new era of globalization can create a kind of "future shock" (Toffler, 1970) to institutions of higher education that have not made active plans to sustain and nurture diverse institutional talent. Clearly, globalization provides a wake-up call to institutions of higher education, signaling the urgent need to address the issue of employee demographics. It also provides an unparalleled opportunity for universities to compete in a global intellectual arena by drawing on the rich potential of diverse American scholars, researchers, and professionals in the educational pipeline. As institutions of higher education create a microcosm reflective of a larger global macrocosm, these efforts require intentional, systemic efforts to actualize the model of demography, diversity, and democracy in campus environments through the framework of reciprocal empowerment.

Although moral arguments about the need for diversity are admirable, larger geopolitical trends driven by economic realities provide an undeniable impetus for change. Yet when discrimination and minimization of talent in the higher education workplace continue unchecked, valued resources and institutional assets are irrevocably lost. The enrichment of an institution's intellectual and creative capital though a workplace that promotes reciprocal empowerment is an enduring investment in viability and excellence. Guided by a theoretical framework that recognizes the impact of sociohistorical forces of exclusion, the next chapter provides a road map to self-assessment of institutional diversity that identifies significant areas of review and a concrete process of measurement.

Mapping the Terrain for Inclusion and Bridging the Gaps

An institution's assessment practices are a reflection of its values.
In other words, the values of an institution are revealed in the
information that it gathers about itself and pays attention to.

[Astin, 1991, p. 3]

TO BEGIN THE PROCESS of institutionwide change in support of
diversity, this chapter focuses on how to identify gaps in diversity progress
through self-assessment of institutionwide diversity. The results of an empirical
and objective self-assessment will generate a clear road map identifying visible
landmarks, invisible barriers, valued protagonists, and strategic opportunities.
A comprehensive institutional self-assessment will prioritize strategic objectives
and will benefit from cross-institutional research to clarify conflicting material
in the diversity literature (Smith and Wolf-Wendel, 2005).

As the first chapter shows, the contemporary pressures of globalization,
shrinking resources, and competitive pressures now demand active efforts to
retain, motivate, and reward diverse talent. Assessment of diversity progress
for public research universities necessarily takes place on a global stage where
interconnection, collaboration, and partnership play leading roles. Universities must "think locally and act globally" (Ulrich, 1998b, p. 126) and serve as
a magnet for talent as well as the glue that holds it together (Kanter, 2003).
As a result, when the institutional self-assessment process is based on the multidimensional framework of demography, diversity, and democracy, the university stands at the crossroads of social change. The integrity of its purposes

is underscored by an approach that embraces the rich reality of democratic pluralism.

Approaches to Diversity Self-Assessment

Institutional self-assessment for diversity needs to examine five major dimensions that provide key measures of progress toward genuine inclusion: (1) structural representation, (2) diversity leadership and strategic focus, (3) organizational learning, (4) behavioral and psychosocial environment, and (5) strategic organizational architecture. To move beyond superficial review and the perpetuation of mere lip service to diversity, institutional self-assessment for diversity must probe more deeply to identify and address the residual forces of domination and oppression that still persist in the context of campus culture, psychosocial environment, and organizational practices. Simply put, the initiation of diversity self-assessment by institutional leadership represents clear recognition that diversity matters.

Several models for diversity assessment situate the major dimensions for cross-institutional evaluation in a progressive framework. One of the most prominent models addresses the evolutionary attainment of diversity in terms of the dimensions of access and success, institutional climate and intergroup relations, education and scholarship, and institutional viability and vitality (Smith, 1995). The groundbreaking Campus Diversity Initiative undertaken in twenty-eight California institutions between 2000 and 2005 relied on this framework as the basis for evaluating diversity (Clayton-Pedersen and others, 2007; Smith, 1995).

In the context of a unifying, overarching framework of assessment, the areas of focus identified for a review of faculty and staff inclusion address the degree to which diversity is embedded in structural practices, organizational culture, and the workplace. The next sections discuss each of these five dimensions in terms of their relationship to reciprocal empowerment and inclusion. Examples of best practices exemplify illustrative strategies that public research universities have developed in these areas.

As a result of the extensive literature that already exists on some of these topics, the focus of this chapter is identification of the most salient elements for consideration in workplace diversity assessment. A sample assessment tool for evaluating diversity progress based on the three-dimensional framework of demography, diversity, and democracy illustrates the concrete application of these themes to the evaluative process (see Appendix A).

Framing the Questions

Relatively little empirical research exists regarding implementation of models of reciprocal empowerment in higher education. Nonetheless, recent insights drawn from diversity research (workplace practices, climate, and structures) coupled with an institution's own demographic analysis can shed light on how demography, diversity, and democracy are actualized in the workplace (Tsui, Egan, and Xin, 1995).

From this perspective, the self-assessment needs to evaluate the extent to which diversity programs are pervasive or localized, central or tangential, and integrated or isolated (Knox and Teraguchi, 2005). Measures of centrality evaluate macrodiversity efforts on campus, including commitment of institutional leadership and creation of diversity infrastructure (Knox and Teraguchi, 2005). Pervasiveness refers to microdiversity initiative or the extent to which programs, including curricular and cocurricular offerings, include diversity (Knox and Teraguchi, 2005). Finally, efforts to assess integration focus on how macro- and microefforts unite to achieve a common institutional vision for diversity (Knox and Teraguchi, 2005).

Selecting the Research Methodology

The approach to assessment benefits from the practitioner-as-researcher model, a form of action inquiry that engages participants in the process of institutional transformation through self-reflection and collaboration (Bensimon, Polkinghorne, Bauman, and Vallejo, 2004). Involving campus stakeholders in the self-study creates buy-in and support for the change. Diversity work then becomes a shared endeavor that engages campus constituents in the three phases of assessment, planning, and action. This form of assessment promotes ownership of outcomes and fosters responsibility and accountability (Clayton-Pedersen and others, 2007). As illustrated by the Diversity Scorecard project undertaken at fourteen urban colleges in California, the involvement of stakeholders in the research is a source of individual and institutional empowerment (Bensimon, Polkinghorne, Bauman, and Vallejo, 2004).

Finding Creative Tension Through Comparative Analysis

The first step in self-assessment is to compare the current state of reciprocal empowerment in the workplace with its intended state. Just as Dr. Martin Luther King identified the positive value of social tension in overcoming racism, so too can organizations move forward through a comparative process of creative tension to attain more inclusive environments (King, 1963; Senge, 2006). Yet the voices of change that have fostered such creative tension in academic communities have often come from those with the least power—students and minorities (Hamilton, 2004). By contrast, when institutional leadership takes on this challenge, attention of all members of the university community is drawn to the work needed to reach the articulated vision.

Beginning the Self-Assessment Interview

To begin the process, the institution will benefit from a self-assessment interview that identifies how the study will proceed and its major objectives. The self-assessment interview can follow step-by-step models that focus on institutional mission such as those developed by the nonprofit Drucker Foundation (Stern, 1999) or by the Campus Diversity Initiative undertaken in California in 2000 to 2005 (Clayton-Pedersen and others, 2007).

Because of its pivotal role in conveying strategic intent and shared values, the mission statement is the rudder that guides the institution forward and stabilizes its course. The Drucker Foundation Self-Assessment Interview uses mission as the linchpin for further analysis (Stern, 1999). Mission lays the groundwork for the determination of long-term goals, objectives that measure levels of achievement, action steps to meet objectives, budget to accomplish these actions, and appraisal to evaluate when results are achieved (Stern, 1999). The centrality of mission coincides with the focus of accreditation processes that measure institutional integrity in terms of how the university fulfills its mission and goals through leveraging its resources and processes (Baker, 2002). Furthermore, programs that exist at the margins of an institution have less impact than those that reflect an institution's examination of diversity as parts of its core mission through functions such as curriculum and academic and career success (Hurtado, 2005).

As a second important tool, the institution's vision statement coalesces future directions and ultimate goals. Successful organizations begin with clearly defined, actionable vision statements that explain the direction the organization is going (Foley, with Kendrick, 2006). Processes and values are drawn from this vision (Foley, with Kendrick, 2006). As a result, if diversity is not a part of the vision statement, operational plans related to diversity remain disconnected from strategic objectives.

For the interview process, questions based on the Drucker Foundation Self-Assessment model provide clear guidelines for change:

Should the institutional mission or vision be revisited in terms of diversity?

What are the institution's overarching diversity goals, and how are they articulated in the mission, vision, or values statement?

What are the most significant diversity challenges in changing the status quo?

What are the most significant opportunities for diversity?

What are the most significant weaknesses of diversity?

What strategies can be developed to address these challenges?

What specific diversity-related results are expected?

What diversity programs need to be strengthened, analyzed, or abandoned?

What will be the institutional outcomes that result from the self-study?

Who will be responsible for specific outcomes?

At the close of the assessment process, the answers to these questions reveal whether initial perceptions coincide with actual findings and where discrepancies exist.

Following the initial interview, separate assessment teams or groups of key stakeholders can undertake each dimension of the analysis, using the practitioner-as-researcher model. These teams benefit from the oversight of a leadership team that ensures coordination of all five assessment activities. A series of foundational questions help to establish the overall parameters of the project and the guidelines for the discrete assessment groups. Sample questions could include:

How will the diversity assessment process relate to the institution's strategic plan and (if applicable) the diversity strategic plan?

What external measurements will help drive the analysis, for example, an environmental scan or the requirements of the regional accreditation processes?

What internal measurements will be used?

How should analysis of the gaps be coordinated or sequenced?

Which major stakeholders or constituencies will be involved in the assessment process and can help bridge the gaps?

What plans and milestones need to be implemented and in what order?

How will the results be used to set future goals?

How will the results be tied to accreditation?

How will organizational learning be enhanced as a result of this work?

What institutional resources will be designated to accomplish specific outcomes?

Measuring the First Dimension: Structural Representation

We now move to a discussion of the specific measurements to be used in the assessment process. Each of the five dimensions represents a different lens or window through which the institution's diversity progress can be measured. The most visible and prominent measure of diversity is the degree of structural representation of women and minorities attained in the workforce. Mechanisms for measuring structural diversity are well established in the research university. The annual affirmative action plan provides a standard, accurate methodology for this aspect of the self-assessment. Based on Executive Order 11246, federal contractors with $50,000 or more of contracts with the federal government must prepare written affirmative action plans with goals and timetables to address any underrepresentation of women and minorities in the workforce. The specific methodology used to determine underutilization compares the statistical availability of women and minorities for specific job groups in the relevant recruitment area with minority and female incumbency in these job groups.

Because clear statutory guidance, considerable research, and a wealth of information exist on affirmative action methodology, the annual affirmative action plan provides a valid and reliable assessment mechanism that allows multiyear comparisons (for more detailed explanation see Crosby, 2004; Evans and Chun, 2007a; U.S. Department of Labor, 2007). The findings of the affirmative action plan are critical for determining whether good-faith efforts have been made to address the hiring and promotion of minority and women faculty and staff.

Despite considerable backlash relating to affirmative action, affirmative action in employment still serves as an important gateway to diversity. Without the hiring of women and minorities, the fundamental attributes of racial, ethnic, and gender diversity will not adequately be represented in the workforce. In this sense, affirmative action and diversity have a synergistic and sequential relationship. The attainment of diversity depends on first attaining structural representation through the recruitment and hiring of women and minorities, followed by systematic efforts to ensure their retention, empowerment, and inclusion (Evans and Chun, 2007a). *Critical mass,* that is, having a sufficient and significant minority presence, is an important institutional objective as it helps dissipate stereotypes about minority groups that arise when few members of such groups are present and fosters a welcoming climate for diversity (Niemann and Maruyama, 2005). As a result, assessment of structural representation necessarily precedes evaluation of later phases of diversity progress.

Diversity Leadership and Strategic Focus

The second dimension of the assessment analysis examines diversity leadership and strategic focus. We discuss the nature and character of diversity leadership and discuss a number of key dimensions with significant institutionwide impact, including leadership by the board of trustees, the president, and the chief diversity officer, and other structural elements such as the diversity strategic plan.

Diversity leadership is multifaceted in the public research university and also includes cabinet-level leadership, governance processes, academic and administrative leadership, campus constituent groups, and participation by faculty and staff labor unions.

Because the sharing of power is an important aspect of reciprocal empowerment, inclusion of women and minorities in leadership roles with actual power rather than in peripheral or token roles is evidence of substantive commitment to diversity. Based on the model of reciprocal empowerment, meaningful inclusion of minorities and women in leadership roles requires voice in decision making (democratic participation), access to resources (distributive justice), and celebration of individual identity (self-determination) (Prilleltensky and Gonick, 1994).

Diversity leadership itself is a distinct form of leadership that addresses diversity issues and concerns in higher education and seeks to adapt to the changing world environment (Aguirre and Martinez, 2006). Diversity leaders serve as change agents in different leadership roles, whether academic or administrative. New diversity leaders, whatever their racial or ethnic identity or gender, need to act on new vision, missions, procedures, and outcomes and be committed to shaping a future that promotes the celebration of cultural democracy (Valverde, 2003). Most important, the diversity leader's objective is to challenge, alter, and restructure institutional policies and practices that advantage or privilege some identities while excluding and marginalizing others (Owen, 2008).

Recognition of the value of diversity leadership may not be present in certain environments. Furthermore, diversity leadership may not be compatible with organizational culture (Aguirre and Martinez, 2006). Because minority leaders in executive roles are rare, the price paid for serving as change agents can be great for these pioneers (Valverde, 2003). Change agents may win battles to lose the overall war—"in the end, they typically lose a great deal, either in the short term, losing their job, or in the long term, hurting their upward mobility and ultimately their careers" (Valverde, 2003, p. 8).

Leadership of the Board of Trustees

Public research universities may be governed by a systemwide board of trustees or by individual boards. For example, in the state of California, the Board of Regents for the University of California oversees ten doctoral/research universities and three laboratories, while the Board of Trustees of the California State University system governs one doctoral/research university, nineteen master's universities, three baccalaureate colleges, and one specialized institution (Hamilton, 2004). By contrast, in the state of Ohio, each public research university has its own board of trustees. Whereas most public boards comprise governors' political appointments, in some states such as North Carolina and Minnesota appointments are made by the legislature (Spanier and Baldwin, 2004). In Nebraska, regents are elected regionally, in Michigan through statewide races (Spanier and Baldwin, 2004).

Diversity among board members is a critical factor in diversity leadership, especially when the chief executive may not share the same level or record of commitment to diversity. In some cases, presidents may be reluctant to tackle crucial issues that may appear controversial, outside the scope of their predominant interests, or beyond their comfort level in terms of their background and expertise (Chait, Holland, and Taylor, 1996). In other cases, the board may have a greater appreciation for imperatives to act such as in initiatives related to globalization (Chait, Holland, and Taylor, 1996). In such cases, the board must motivate the president to attend to these directions, as trustees play an instrumental role in the attainment of desired institutional outcomes (Chait, Holland, and Taylor, 1996). Although boards hold a great deal in trust in terms of the institution's reputation, human resources, and financial assets, the most precious asset entrusted to the board is the institution's values (Chait, Holland, and Taylor, 1993).

Two surveys conducted by the Association of Governing Boards of Universities and Colleges in 2004 found that 21 percent of the nation's estimated ten thousand public college trustees were members of minority groups (Fain, 2005). Yet although boards are becoming more racially diverse, they still have fewer minority members compared with college enrollments and the general population (Fain, 2005). Especially underrepresented among board members are Asian Americans and Hispanic Americans (Fain, 2005).

The board of trustees typically has responsibility for hiring the president and evaluating presidential candidates in terms of their track record with respect to diversity as well as the degree to which candidates have created an open and welcoming environment in prior positions. A past track record of progress in affirmative action and diversity initiatives is an important indicator of the commitment of candidates to inclusion.

Because trustees play an instrumental role in the formulation of institutional direction, they can insist on the creation of policies, programs, and processes that support diversity and globalization as well as a respectful and empowering work environment. For example, the Board of Trustees of Eastern Washington University initiated a broad-based diversity initiative in 2002. The explicit goal of the trustees' initiative is "to build a stronger community that is inclusive, respectful, and supportive of all of its members; a community that celebrates its diversity and its unity; a community that expects honesty; and that provides an environment for safe interaction among its members" (Eastern Washington University, 2008, para. 1). President and vice presidents were specifically charged with leadership and to report to the board on funding for the project, engagement of external experts for a climate survey, and collaboration with a faculty fellow accountable to the vice presidents collectively (Eastern Washington University, 2002).

Presidential Leadership

One of the most critical factors in successful diversity in higher education is committed and visible presidential leadership. Presidential leadership creates a framework that allows constituents to connect to the shared values of the institution (Birnbaum, 1992). Presidents can draw on existing campus leadership, faculty support, and other key constituents in developing and articulating a vision of diversity change. They also have the opportunity to set expectations for concrete action and outcomes, stimulate instrumental workplace support for the success of minority and female administrators and faculty, build a strong and diverse administrative team, provide institutional resources, and institutionalize structures that will perpetuate diversity progress.

Although presidents must actively build collaboration and support for policy and cultural changes, they can affect the moral, political, and social climate of a campus, sensitize trustees and alumni to diversity issues, signal visible commitment to constituent groups, and insist on change at the executive level (Brown, 1998). Yet transformational leadership that emphasizes values and goals, advances new cultural forms, and moves campuses to higher levels of motivation and morality is more the exception than the rule (Birnbaum, 1992). Presidents are usually conservative and may not wish to revolutionize a system in which they have succeeded (Birnbaum, 1992).

Relatively few university presidents embody the diversity demanded by global society (Jackson, 2008). Over the past two decades, the percentage of minority college and university presidents has increased only slightly, from 8.1 percent to 13.5 percent (Bridges, Eckel, Cordova, and White, 2008). If minority-serving institutions are excluded from this number, minority presidents lead less than 10 percent of institutions (Bridges, Eckel, Cordova, and White, 2008). Women have made greater advances, with representation rising from 10 percent to 23 percent over the past two decades, although they are much less likely to lead doctorate-granting institutions (Bridges, Eckel, Cordova, and White, 2008). Because 40 percent of presidents arose from chief academic officer, greater diversification of CAO positions is important, particularly for Asian Americans who represent only 2 percent of CAOs and 3 percent of deans (King and Gomez, 2008).

Characteristics of Effective Diversity Leadership

The revolution in leadership research during the past twenty years has moved away from value-neutral, highly structured, and hierarchical leadership models to globalized and process-focused views of leadership to models that identify the importance of cross-cultural understanding, interdependence, collaboration, and empowerment (Kezar, Carducci, and Contreras-McGavin, 2006). Democratic practices and autonomy indicate an environment of empowerment (Kezar, Carducci, and Contreras-McGavin, 2006). Characteristics of effective pluralistic leadership include understanding different cultural norms; cultivating diverse viewpoints; emphasizing self-awareness; being open to new processes, styles, and experiences; and desiring individual and collective growth (Kezar, 2001).

An important perspective on diversity leadership is provided by positionality theory, which identifies not only the social construction of power but also the ways in which individuals relate to these conditions based on individual background, identity, experience, and other contextual factors (Kezar, 2000). From an institutional standpoint, invisible historical legacies and structural contexts still situate individuals and groups differently in the power structure (Maher and Tetreault, 2007). These legacies can perpetuate the continuation of white privilege that has both historically and contemporaneously shaped power relations and resulted in systematic inequality (Kincheloe and Steinberg, 1998). Experiences of these legacies of power influence not only how individual diversity leaders approach their roles but also their potential ability to effect change.

For example, interviews with three African American women presidents revealed that these leaders felt that expectations were higher than for their white male counterparts and cited the difficulty subordinates had in accepting them in positions of authority (Lindsay, 1999). Despite their high rank, acceptance of an "outsider" as president meant that these individuals had a far different experience of presidential leadership than their majority counterparts. As diversity leaders, they were challenged differently because of their place in the organization and the historical legacies and images that accompanied perceptions of diverse leadership. To overcome these perceptions, their leadership style might require different attributes such as a greater tendency to collaboration and consensus building, the ability to neutralize criticism, and greater subtlety in managing institutional processes.

Diversity Strategic Focus

An important aspect of diversity leadership assessment addresses the extent to which an institution has incorporated diversity into its strategic planning and goals. Research on competitive strategy in major American corporations provides valuable guidance on the relationship of strategic focus to organizational success. This research links the following factors to increased organizational success that can be applied to diversity strategic focus: (1) leveraging resources in pursuit of seemingly unattainable goals; (2) accelerating organizational learning to build new competitive advantage and outpace competitors; (3) digesting a single challenge at a time before launching the next; (4) building competitive intelligence at every level of the organization; and (5) engaging employees intellectually and emotionally in meeting institutional challenges and developing new skills (Hamel and Prahalad, 1989).

As discussed earlier, evaluation of an institution's diversity strategic focus begins with the mission statement and then considers how the mission is embraced and translated into workplace realities. In this process, the dichotomy and distance between the perceived and real image of the university increase when mission statements are not actualized (Fenelon, 2003). Acceptance of institutional mission by campus stakeholders is not automatic: time and effort are involved in socializing individuals to the mission and ensuring that it is reinforced on public occasions and in meetings and conversations (Kezar, 2005a).

Findings from the California-based Campus Diversity Initiative (2000–2005) reveal that when senior leadership understood the linkage between diversity and institutional vitality, campuses were more successful in actualizing diversity mission statements (Clayton-Pedersen and others, 2007). As a result, programmatic efforts to embed the mission statement and principles in institutional culture benefit from a prospective and proactive approach that connects diversity to institutional success.

Diversity Strategic Plans

The presence of a diversity strategic plan is a leading-edge best practice that clearly reflects executive sponsorship of the change process. In part because of factors such as size and the importance of federal funding, public research universities have been in the forefront of the development of diversity strategic plans and have recognized the importance of these plans as a driving and persuasive force in the change process (Evans and Chun, 2007a).

Critical elements of diversity strategic plans include specific designation of accountability, budget and infrastructure, assessment, channels for collective campus input, and concrete objectives and time lines. Yet relatively few such plans include comprehensive efforts to move beyond affirmative action and structural representation to reciprocal empowerment (Evans and Chun, 2007a).

An insightful study of twenty-one diversity action plans at twenty land-grant institutions over a period of five years (Iverson, 2008) identifies dominant discourses that frame the discussion of diversity:

Discourses of access and disadvantage that portray diverse individuals as outsiders to the university and at risk once they enter the institution. These discourses include distinct strands focused on entry, representation, and affirmation.

A marketplace discourse that emphasizes multicultural competence in the context of rapidly changing global conditions. This discourse includes distinct strands focused on excellence through quality, performance, and reputation as well as managerialism with an emphasis on accountability and effectiveness.

A discourse of democracy that focuses on inclusion and opportunity, open dialogue, civic responsibility, and commitment to equity.

A discourse of reciprocal empowerment falls logically in the discourse of democracy. An example of a diversity plan that addresses reciprocal empowerment is Diversity Blueprints Final Report from the University of Michigan (2007). The plan emphasizes in its opening statement that "diversity is the experience of meaningful exploration and exchange through a set of dynamic and reciprocal interactions" (p. 2). Furthermore, the Michigan report focuses on the *actions* of diversity and proposes recommendations dealing with structural accountability, rewards, remediation of barriers, and the creation of expansive opportunities for interaction (University of Michigan, 2007). The university's explicit recognition that diversity is embedded in the character of interaction and reciprocity represents a significant institutional best practice.

The Chief Diversity Officer as a Structural Best Practice

One of the emerging preeminent best practices regarding diversity leadership is the establishment of a chief diversity officer position reporting to the president or provost and holding significant institutional rank such as vice president or vice provost. A national study of these positions identifies three organizational archetypes for the chief diversity officer: a collaborative officer with little formal power in terms of staff or direct supervision; a unit-based model with greater vertical authority; and a portfolio divisional model that integrates the diversity leadership structure for multiple units under a single unit (Williams and Wade-Golden, 2007a). To expand institutional capacity for diversity, chief diversity officers can assist in a number of core areas such as interfacing with institutional accountability processes, building diversity infrastructure, infusing diversity in the curriculum, and elevating the visibility and credibility of diversity efforts (Williams and Wade-Golden, 2007b).

Development of Diversity Scorecards and Similar Assessment Tools

Because the academic mission is critical to the realization of inclusive excellence, evaluative and diagnostic tools that reflect the institutions' characteristics can be developed (Anderson, 2007). An academic mission scorecard developed by Anderson (2007) evaluates behaviors and actions of academic officers that support diversity, including leadership in areas of campus climate, the ability to engage faculty in critical discourse on diversity, and involvement in decision making.

When diversity and inclusion are not referenced as part of the institution's core work, the likelihood decreases that prioritization will be given to diversity in terms of short- and long-term strategic planning, resource allocation, and structural change. Based on the assessment framework discussed in this chapter, a sample planning tool for assessment of diversity leadership is presented in Appendix A. This tool references the three-dimensional model of demography, diversity, and democracy and draws on recent research models to align intentions with practices (Musil, 2006).

Organizational Learning

The third dimension of the self-assessment process measures the scope and effectiveness of organizational learning undertaken by the institution in support of diversity. We examine how organizational learning provides a major vehicle for attaining the institution's vision and mission for diversity and how it is intertwined in the core work of the institution.

Ironically, the concept of organizational learning may seem foreign in the academic environment, an environment that often focuses on individual scholarship and attainment. Whereas faculty serve as knowledge creators for their professions, they are frequently not empowered, called on, or engaged in the creation of knowledge for their own institution's learning processes (White and Weathersby, 2005). The rigors of academic life often engender competition, autonomy, intellectual skepticism, and the need to focus on individual interests, factors that may run counter to the process of organizational learning (White and Weathersby, 2005). Nonetheless, research universities typically possess a powerhouse of talent in their own walls that can be used to spark and sustain the diversity organizational learning process.

Despite limited recognition of its value and significance, organizational learning is one of the most powerful levers for accomplishing transformational change in support of reciprocal empowerment. Organizational learning enhances institutional effectiveness, as it touches on the institution's core work, encourages use of common structures for reflecting on process and results, involves cross-institutional stakeholders, is internally driven, and builds on the accepted academic paradigm of educational effectiveness (Smith and Parker, 2005).

In this regard, theorists view organizational learning as distinctly different from the concept of a learning organization developed by Senge (1990) and others, because it refers to a systematic body of research that studies how and under what conditions organizations learn and change (Kezar, 2005b). Yet organizational learning capabilities are difficult to attain as organizational learning far exceeds the boundaries of individual learning (Argyris and others, 1994). Individual learning is a necessary but not sufficient condition for organizationwide learning (Argyris and others, 1994). Organizational learning requires that a critical mass of individuals in the institution operate in new ways, leading to the establishment of infrastructures that support learning as well as new organizational norms and habits (Argyris and others, 1994).

Collaborative learning in the university blurs the lines between traditional conceptions of teaching, service, and research and represents forms of engagement in which knowledge is shared, interpreted, and applied collaboratively (Ramaley, 2006). In this sense, engagement through collaborative learning is a lens through which life and work come together and in which the broader community plays an active role (Ramaley, 2006).

The observation that organizational learning occurs when an institutional culture changes its range of potential behaviors has special significance for the diversity assessment process (Huber, 1991). The five-year Campus Diversity Initiative in California provides a clear research-based model of how to accomplish institutionwide diversity progress through organizational learning. Rather than simply focusing on diversity as an end goal related to representation among faculty, staff, and students, the project required campus leaders to understand diversity as an opportunity for organizational learning linked to institutional mission

(Clayton-Pedersen and others, 2007; Smith and Parker, 2005). This systems-based approach connects mission and diversity through the medium of organizational learning.

New Designs and Mental Models for Organizational Learning

How can effective organizational learning be generated in support of diversity? An important requirement for change involves the mapping of new designs and mental models both individually and institutionally that will lead to effective action (Argyris, 1993). The principal barriers to change are "brain barriers"—preexisting, successful mental maps (Black and Gregersen, 2002). Organizational defensive patterns will not be altered by structural changes such as creating policies or reward systems if individuals do not have the skills or mindsets to reduce organizational defenses (Argyris, 1993). Furthermore, when an issue such as diversity activates embarrassment or threat, systematic discrepancies develop between how individuals espouse dealing effectively with others and the actual theory they use (Argyris, 1997). Counterproductive defensive routines that limit learning may come into play—unilateral control, striving to win and not lose, suppression of negative feelings, and an emphasis on being as rational as possible, for example (Argyris, 1997).

A psychodynamic view of organizational learning reveals that organizations as well as individuals are not generally motivated to learn when learning involves "anxiety-producing identity change" (Brown and Starkey, 2000, p. 102). Organizations, like individuals, maintain collective self-esteem by not questioning existing self-concepts or identity (Brown and Starkey, 2000). As a result, institutions of higher education may resort to implementing co-optative strategies to diversity that result in lip service or window dressing through tokenism rather than changing the existing culture (Aguirre and Martinez, 2006).

Organizational learning that addresses reciprocal empowerment requires the introduction of new designs, mind-sets, and forms of institutional understanding. Such learning also must take into account issues of power and trust in a context of subcultures that may not be homogenous (Easterby-Smith, Crossan, and Nicolini, 2000). Models of organizational learning that are tailored to the realities of a given institutional culture and emphasize collaboration and sense making have been shown to have greater success in the change process (Kezar and Eckel, 2002).

The locus of responsibility and infrastructure for organizational learning is shifting to the everyday experiences and activities of the workplace (Argyris and others, 1994). In contrast with the notion of separate, stand-alone training activities, diversity learning is an integrated activity that occurs constantly on a daily basis. In this sense, it is infused with the work and inseparable from the work (Argyris and others, 1994). Diversity learning is intertwined with job content, roles, and responsibilities. Because learning unfolds daily, the role of training and development professionals now must focus on partnerships with those accountable for the issues being addressed (Argyris and others, 1994). Faculty expertise is an often neglected resource that is essential in guiding these new forms of learning.

Furthermore, diversity organizational learning also takes place through informal structures such as coalitions, work teams, or study groups that include multicultural participation. These multicultural coalitions or study groups can heighten awareness of the subtle ways in which white privilege operates using practical tools such as the twenty-five assumptions of privilege developed by Crowfoot and Chesler (1996).

The Scarcity of Best Practice Examples

Few examples can be found of comprehensive, long-term, systemic diversity organizational learning programs that address cultural change in public research universities. As Patricia Digh, cofounder of the Global Diversity Roundtable and the Circle Project, points out, the nature of "wicked problems and tame solutions" is that Americans prefer short-term, quick, and linear approaches to diversity and racism (*Chronicle of Higher Education,* 2007). Merely scheduling a two-hour workshop on diversity can be a tame solution imposed on a wicked problem that obscures its nature and then draws on linear methods for resolution (*Chronicle of Higher Education,* 2007). To resist the impulse to tidiness, institutions need to step back to contemplate the complexity of the problem and to understand, like a Rubik's cube, how change in one aspect affects other parts of the problem (*Chronicle of Higher Education,* 2007).

An example of a program that focuses on organizational learning in support of diversity is the Diversity Education Program at the University of California at Davis. This program has high-level leadership and assigned resources as well as curricular offerings that address cultural competence, multicultural leadership, and diversity awareness (University of California, Davis, 2007). At the University of Illinois, the Center on Democracy in a Multiracial Society, formed in 2002, focuses on research that will open discussions on race to improve campus climate among the university's more than forty-one thousand students, faculty, and staff (Chew, 2008). Formed at the suggestion of Professor Joe Feagin, the center's agenda includes efforts to realize the benefits of diversity, form coalitions, and empower members of the university community to participate more effectively in a diverse workplace (University of Illinois at Urbana-Champaign, 2002).

The Power of Institutional Culture

The fourth dimension of the self-assessment analysis focuses on organizational culture, climate, and psychosocial environment. This section discusses methods of cultural and climate assessment that will illuminate the degree to which the university environment is welcoming and inclusive.

In this era of globalization, American corporations have become increasingly aware of the influence of the culture of the organization on success and excellence. Globalization demands that organizations pay attention to the "soft stuff" such as culture change and the management of diversity, complexity, and ambiguity to be competitive (Ulrich, 1998b). Similarly, in higher education, psychological climate, behavioral dimensions, and an institution's historical legacy of inclusion or exclusion have a direct effect on institutional quality, engagement, and success (Hurtado, Milem, Clayton-Pedersen, and Allen, 1999; Smith and Wolf-Wendel, 2005).

Although assessment of the psychosocial environment in higher education is a difficult and challenging process, the behavioral and cultural environment is the critical testing ground for the presence or absence of reciprocal empowerment. In the microcosm of daily experience, the concrete interactions experienced by female and minority faculty and staff reflect whether they are included or excluded, supported or marginalized, given voice or silenced. Subtle forms of twenty-first-century discrimination demand careful attention to microincursions or the small, cumulative acts of exclusion that can lead to more significant consequences in retention, career growth, and job satisfaction.

Because the academic cultural terrain suggests "a constricted democratic practice where the very act of living can reside on the margins" (Padilla and Chávez, 1995, p. 7), how minority and female faculty and staff function in a given environment and how they perceive themselves are important considerations in cultural self-assessment (Hurtado, 1996). Because of the subjective nature of the practice of democracy as it transpires through personal agency and the interplay in everyday environments (Padilla and Chávez, 1995), the ways in which individual experiences shape and are shaped by the culture provide invaluable qualitative perspectives in the assessment.

Culture and Climate

A clear goal of the self-assessment is to unveil the assumptions, norms, and tacit beliefs hidden below the surface of the work environment. The tip of the proverbial cultural iceberg is not sufficient for such an analysis. The analysis must determine when and how the stated values of the institution in support of diversity are not congruent with the operating values of the institution (Foley, with Kendrick, 2006).

From the standpoint of definition, culture is the medium through which behavior is transmitted; it reflects behavioral, emotional, and cognitive dimensions of how the group functions from a psychological perspective (Schein, 1992). Culture embodies the deeply held values that are not easily changed and that govern ways of thinking, acting, and resolving problems (Peterson and Spencer, 1990; Schein, 1992). The concept of climate, in contrast, refers to a more temporal phenomenon—a fluctuating and transient reflection of organizational life.

Because of the difficulty of identifying hidden cultural assumptions relating to diversity, survival and success for women and minorities in the academy have been described in terms of "ontological holograms" (Padilla and Chávez, 1995). The differing facets of the cultural hologram do not reveal themselves until held up to the light. In addition, minority and women faculty and staff may in fact contribute to these hidden assumptions through collusion or hegemony—the process by which dominant groups attain the consensus of those whom they rule—affecting the experiences of everyday life in academe (Padilla and Chávez, 1995).

Diversity work that incorporates a strong evaluative approach—and by extension that touches on cultural assumptions—inevitably faces considerable resistance (Clayton-Pedersen and others, 2007). Specific types of resistance as demonstrated in the Campus Diversity Initiative were fear, clandestine or "stealth" resistance, suspicion about the evaluation and assessment process, concerns about emerging legal trends, and anxiety about public scrutiny (Clayton-Pedersen and others, 2007).

Methods of Cultural Assessment

Although surveys have been a frequently used method of assessing institutional climate, culture questionnaires are not sufficient to reveal cultural assumptions as culture covers what an organization has learned over its history as well as the tacit assumptions individuals hold (Schein, 2006). Even to begin such a survey, one would not know what to ask about or what questions to design (Schein, 2006). A qualitative approach is needed that will touch on the deeper layers of tacit assumptions and unspoken cultural norms and engage individuals in dialogue regarding the institution's mission, vision, and values. Without an explicit focus, such an exercise can be fruitless and adds little value (Schein, 2006).

Interviews that compare an institution's stated values with its operating values (Foley, with Kendrick, 2006) provide a starting point for addressing incongruencies in how the organization works. Such interviews and discussion require careful facilitation, expert guidance, and confidentiality because of the need to surface hidden assumptions and subtexts. The potential for extremely polarized views about diversity and the depth of disagreement that typically surfaces around this issue make skillful facilitation a necessity.

As part of the interview process, participation from administrators, faculty, and staff from different organizational areas, positions, and backgrounds in the institution provides needed insight into the values and views of internal stakeholders. Analysis of the normative influence of different subcultures in a given institution is an essential part of the process. For example, the climate for diversity can vary from department to department, resulting in a patchwork of microclimates—cool in one area and warm in another. In this regard, a study of 437 staff at a large, predominantly white public university in the Midwest revealed that staff members who perceived their department to be supportive of diversity were more likely to report that their institutional community had a positive climate for diversity (Mayhew, Grunwald, and Dey, 2006).

Because the goal of cultural assessment is to initiate transformational change, the leadership of human resource professionals can help guide a process that involves defining and clarifying the concept of cultural change, articulating why culture change is critical for organizational success, and identifying alternate approaches to creating culture change (Ulrich, 1998b).

Climate Studies

A study of campus climate is the most prevalent institutional barometer used to gauge diversity in public research universities, as evidenced by the rapid growth of these studies in recent years. Arguably, if an institution has not undertaken a climate study, it will be unlikely to make progress in diversity. A report prepared as a result of the formation of a universitywide study group on diversity at the University of California, Los Angeles (2005) indicates that diversity initiatives remain incomplete unless campus climate is not only acknowledged but also monitored and measured regularly across all departments and disciplines (University of California, 2007). The report emphasizes that intentional institutional action must be taken to monitor climate issues.

Design of the survey needs to address the following considerations: (1) tailoring the survey to the specific institutional environment; (2) determining how results will be used; (3) identifying what data will be useful; (4) concentrating on the appropriate content such as information, behavior, or attitudes; (5) not trying to do too much; and (6) recognizing the limitations of the data (Sedlacek, 2000). A number of higher education surveys focus on rapidly disappearing forms of overt discrimination such as disparaging remarks or blatant behavior without testing the waters for subtle forms of twenty-first-century discrimination. To address the presence or absence of reciprocal empowerment, the climate study benefits from exploration of how individuals of diverse backgrounds are valued, what resources are made available to them, how knowledge is shared with them, and how their initiative is supported (Smith and Sadler-Smith, 2006).

To obtain an overview of different approaches to survey development, representative resources can be found on the comprehensive Web site developed by the Provost's Office at the University of Wisconsin–Madison as well as in other publications (University of Wisconsin–Madison, 2007; see also "Campus Climate Reports," 2002; Garcia and others, 2001; Shenkle, Snyder, and Bauer, 1998). Although some climate studies focus only on student experiences, many have drawn extensively on faculty and staff perceptions in measuring overall climate. The interrelationship of administrative, faculty, and staff climate with student success and student perceptions of racial relations is an important consideration in the evaluation of campus climate. For example, as a study of nearly twenty-five hundred students at 116 predominantly white institutions revealed, institutional commitment to diversity can measurably improve minority perceptions of race relations on campus and also, to some extent, white student perceptions (Hurtado, 1996). Conversely, institutions may foster racial tension when priorities work against promotion of a better climate (Hurtado, 1996).

A prominent example of a faculty job satisfaction survey is the survey conducted by the Collaborative on Academic Careers in Higher Education (2007), a project sponsored by the Ford Foundation at Harvard University's Graduate School of Education, which examined aspects of the climate, culture, and collegiality of the workplace by drawing on a sample of 6,773 tenure-track faculty members at seventy-seven institutions. The survey underscored the lower job satisfaction among female faculty than male faculty and the fact that minority faculty gave all climate aspects lower ratings than did their white counterparts.

Best Practice Examples in Climate Studies

A best practice example that illustrates how to evaluate the presence of reciprocal empowerment in the everyday working environment is the comprehensive climate survey conducted by Stony Brook University in 2004–2005 (State University of New York, Stony Brook, 2005) followed immediately by a significant action plan to address the results (State University of New York, Stony Brook, 2006).

The initial study was designed by an advisory committee representing non-majority populations who are typically underrepresented. The survey identified five dimensions of overall campus climate: acceptance and inclusion, equality and equity, respect, diversity, and safety. It was connected to mandatory diversity training, and respondents were asked to evaluate training topics as part of the survey. Faculty advisors provided research insights into the survey development. The substantive sample of 2,266 employees provided a solid base of data for analysis, and specific questions were asked in terms of respect, sense of support from colleagues and supervisors, inclusion, and representation in policy-making groups (State University of New York, Stony Brook, 2005). To follow up on the survey findings, a subcommittee on participation and empowerment recommended the formation of a campus climate response team to identify systemic patterns as well as individual situations of disempowerment (2006).

Other effective climate survey instruments, including those developed by the National Initiative for Leadership and Effectiveness, a consortium founded at the University of Texas, Austin in 1990 to study the interaction of leadership and organizational culture, have been used to determine existing campus climate (Sullivan, Reichard, and Shumate, 2005). In particular, the Personal Assessment of the College Environment has been used at seven universities since 1989 and has allowed the initiative to develop national norms that provide feedback on leadership models ranging from coercive to collaborative (Sullivan, Reichard, and Shumate, 2005).

Strategic Organizational Architecture for Diversity

The final component of the self-assessment examines the institution's organizational architecture in terms of the degree to which institutional systems, structures, policies, and practices align strategically to promote reciprocal empowerment and inclusion. This dimension of the self-assessment focuses on how structures, systems, and organizational capabilities support the institutionalization of diversity and inclusion.

Organizational architecture involves the creation of a framework for the organization of the future that includes all formal and informal systems and their interaction (Silverman, 1997). This framework guides institutionwide efforts, focusing on both the content and process of large-scale change (Silverman, 1997). The planning process benefits from the expertise of human resource change agents who apply organizational development approaches to promote transformative change. A study of more than twenty thousand human resource professionals over a decade identified five core competencies of human resource professionals that contributed to organizational effectiveness: deep business knowledge, effective delivery of human resource practices, ability to manage change, culture management, and personal credibility (Brockbank, Ulrich, and Beatty, 1999). The study found that the ability to manage change was more important than delivery of human resource practices and business knowledge combined (Brockbank, Ulrich, and Beatty, 1999). Based on the results of this comprehensive study, high-performing human resource professionals can play an instrumental role in facilitating cultural change. A later study of four hundred companies completed by Ulrich, Brockbank, Johnson, and Younger in 2007 amplifies these findings by identifying the organizational designer and cultural steward as core human resource roles (Grossman, 2007).

Human resource functions in higher education are frequently bifurcated, with separate responsibility for academic personnel processes such as promotion and tenure review on the academic side of the house and benefits, labor relations, compensation, employment, and records on the finance side. Despite the separation of these processes, academic and human resource personnel must work together to fashion a unified approach that ensures greater strategic impact and effectiveness in support of cultural change and diversity planning.

The modification of existing systems and structures in support of diversity requires links to human resource systems such as compensation, performance evaluation, and communication (Ulrich, 1998b). As a result, strategic integration of diversity in other institutional systems includes diversity as a *formal* component of management systems linked with other components of "business" strategy such as finance and marketing (Cox, 2001).

From this perspective, an overall evaluation of human resource processes with respect to diversity benefits from a scorecard approach such as the HR Scorecard (Becker, Huselid, and Ulrich, 2001), the Diversity Scorecard (Hubbard, 2004), or the Structural Representation Scorecard (Chun, 2004; cited in Evans and Chun, 2007a).

In the development of an integrated human resources and diversity strategy, two key criteria need to be considered that might initially seem contradictory. First, institutional programs and policies that foster democratic inclusion must offer the potential for success for all members of the community (Thomas, 1990). This aspect of human resource strategic planning recognizes the pitfalls of polarization around issues of race and gender. Second, while the research university must remedy the underrepresentation of minorities and women, it must move beyond this initial stage to promote a culture of inclusion.

Structural Components in the Institutionalization of Diversity

An effective change model for diversity requires the incorporation of diversity in structural processes and organizational practices to ensure long-term sustainable results. Diversity cannot be implemented without changing the institution's underlying structure and day-to-day operations (Brayboy, 2003). Specifically, organizational architecture, design, and reward structures are the vehicles that can actualize diversity as a core value. For example, the formation of a diversity council or diversity cabinet of faculty, administrators, and staff that reports directly to the president or provost is a strategic and structural approach that creates broad, campuswide synergy and accountability for the progress of diversity. Such a body needs to be empowered to make effective recommendations for action. Follow-up by the administration on recommendations and findings creates credibility. For example, the University of Washington's Diversity Council, formed in 2001, comprises representatives from faculty, staff, and student constituencies as well as representatives from each major administrative area and constituent groups (University of Washington, 2009). The council addresses institutionwide diversity at all three campuses and addresses issues of diversity in curriculum, climate, outreach, research, and faculty and student recruitment.

The university's governance structure also presents significant opportunities for minorities and women to engage in the formulation of institutional policies and preferences (Aguirre and Martinez, 2006). In this regard, for example, the University of Wisconsin–Madison's diversity plan includes letters of support from campus governance leaders as well as information on the diversity initiatives of specific shared governance committees (McCown, 2008).

The Value of a Comprehensive Talent Strategy

As articulated in the six key principles in the first chapter, a comprehensive talent strategy assists the institution through recruitment and retention processes that foster diversity and inclusiveness and ensure the attainment of structural representation. Talent management refers to institutional practices designed to attract, retain, and develop the workforce and is recognized as the principal driver of organizational success (Lockwood, 2006). Leading professional associations such as the Society for Human Resource Management and other prominent consulting firms have developed specific surveys on talent management (Lockwood, 2006). According to the society's 2006 Talent Management Survey Report, more than half of the 384 human resource professionals responding indicated that their organizations had specific talent management strategies in place, with areas of improvement identified as creating a culture that retains employees, identifying gaps in competency levels, creating policies that encourage professional development, and building succession plans (Fegley, 2006).

Diversity recruitment has become an increasing focus of talent management in the higher education literature. A growing array of resources provides clear guidance and insights on specific diversity recruitment strategies pertinent to faculty and staff. These resources focus on strengthening outreach, marketing the institution as an employer of choice, eliminating bias in hiring processes through diverse search committees and structured interviewing processes, using technology, and holding stakeholders accountable for the attainment of equity and affirmative action goals (see, for example Moody, 2004; Turner, 2002).

Retention is also a key consideration in the development of talent management strategies. As a result, the self-assessment needs to address the extent to which the institution has developed an effective program for retention of diverse faculty and staff. Such a program should include analysis of turnover through quantitative and qualitative data, use of exit interview findings, policy development, work-life strategies, professional development and mentoring, compensation programs, and rewards for diversity contributions. Such processes will foster employees' engagement and increase their job satisfaction.

As part of the evaluative framework related to retention, the Employee Value Proposition provides a model for first identifying and then communicating to employees the important factors that contribute to retention (Ledford, 2002). This approach specifically references the elements of work content, institutional affiliation, indirect and direct financials, and career development as components of the proposition (Ledford, 2002). Diversity also needs to be a key component in an institution's employee value proposition. Because talent is attracted to conditions where diversity and tolerance are greater (Florida, 2002a), the degree to which diversity is reflected in formal institutional arrangements and valued in the day-to-day context of departmental life affects the long-term retention of diverse talent.

Policies and Procedures

Formal policies and procedures provide the essential structural and organizational framework that can drive progress in diversity, eliminate discriminatory practices, foster retention, and ensure equity, organizational justice, and consistency. Specific areas for policy review related to diversity include recruitment and hiring policies; merit review processes; tenure and promotion processes; leave policies, including work-life provisions and provisions regarding the tenure clock; disciplinary policies; and equity, nondiscrimination, and complaint policies.

Even when specific policies have been created that appear to support diversity practices, the self-assessment also needs to address the degree to which policies are operationalized and protections exist for those who access policy provisions. A rather startling finding of a survey by the Collaborative on Academic Careers in Higher Education (2007) indicates that even when policies exist that create support structures for female and minority faculty and staff, they may be perceived as ineffective.

Human Resource Capabilities Audit

Evaluation of the institution's organizational architecture benefits from implementation of a human resource capabilities audit. Such an audit is focused on whether the institution possesses the necessary capabilities in its workforce to realize its strategic goals. Organizational capabilities are the intangible assets that the institution possesses—the collective expertise, abilities, and skills that give an institution its *identity* (Ulrich and Smallwood, 2004). These capabilities reside in the systems, overall design, and culture of the institution, are difficult to duplicate, and are a source of competitive advantage that differentiates institutions (Lawler, 2006).

Development of the requisite competencies in the workforce is necessary to actualize the critical organizational capability of diversity. Hiring and selection criteria that accentuate the necessary skills, expertise, and attributes for collaboration and inclusion contribute to this organizational capability. Based on the assessment tool developed by Ulrich and Smallwood (2004), an organizational capabilities audit helps to identify the relationship of factors such as talent, speed, shared mind-set, creativity, collaboration, leadership, and organizational learning to diversity. Sample questions for the audit based on Ulrich and Smallwood's tool (2004) include:

Do diversity results matter, and are they directed toward the execution of institutional strategy?

Are new ideas for diversity generated across institutional subboundaries?

Do employees have an intellectual, behavioral, and procedural agenda for attaining inclusion and reciprocal empowerment?

Do we reduce redundancy in diversity programming through efficient management of processes?

Concluding Observations

At this pivotal time in history, the survival of our planet and of the United States as a democratic nation depends on knowledge, talent, and creativity. Without unleashing the contributions of a diverse faculty and staff, universities will fail to mine the precious resources that can contribute to our collective survival.

Why is assessment of the gaps in diversity progress an essential step in the process of cultural change and institutional transformation? A persuasive approach to assessment serves as a catalyst to inclusion and reciprocal empowerment for faculty and staff. Diversity self-assessment, like other institutional assessment processes, is often put on a back burner, because it is time consuming, viewed as a distraction without immediate results, and is frequently politically charged. Given the major impetus of globalization, institutional diversity assessment provides the ability for an institution to connect its mission and vision with its actions through the lens of reciprocal empowerment. Recognition of the university as a diversity leader that means what it says and enacts what it promises fosters synergy with both internal and external stakeholders. Actions that transform the campus environment in support of diversity build reputation, connect the institution's values and practices, strengthen employee retention, and ensure long-term competitiveness in the search for talent. This progressive focus actualizes the uniquely American vision of participation, inclusion, and the democratic distribution of power in the fabric of university life.

Orchestrating the Process of Cultural Change

> Whereas strategy is abstract and based on long-term goals, tactics are concrete and based on finding the best move right now. Tactics are conditional and opportunistic, all about threat and defense.
>
> [Kasparov, 2007, p. 16]

ONCE LONG-TERM DIVERSITY GOALS have been established through self-assessment, the next major phase in the attainment of reciprocal empowerment requires the skilled and balanced orchestration of cultural change through concrete tactical strategies. Tactics are fluid. As long ago as 500 B.C., the Chinese philosopher Sun-Tzu wrote, "No one victory is gained in the same manner as another. The tactics change in an infinite variety of ways to suit changes in the circumstances" (Michaelson, 2007, p. 22). Designing the tactics for change *is* rocket science, for change is complex and nonlinear and needs to provide the potential for creative breakthroughs (Fullan, 2001).

Diversity management is a craft comprising the knowledge and skills necessary to achieve success (R. R. Thomas, 2006). It is also an art. Designers of change need to carefully deploy the appropriate array of tactics, skills, and knowledge needed to build consensus and achieve diversity. Tactical approaches must effectively use the elements of time, speed, and resources to accomplish institutional objectives. Flexibility, mobility, and a balancing of elements are essential (Kasparov, 2007). Tactical execution demands innovation, creativity, and resourceful planning to anticipate and overcome barriers and ensure the successive, phased attainment of results.

The opposing dialectic implicit in the comparison between the frameworks of systemic racism and reciprocal empowerment shared in "Translating Principles into Practice" is also present in the balancing of tactical factors needed to accomplish change such as by recognizing complexity but staying on its "far side" (Fullan, 2008, p. 130) or coordinating a sophisticated blend of top-down and bottom-up strategies (Fullan, 1994). Flexibility in execution needs to be coupled with focused attention on desired outcomes.

Because cultural change is neither quick nor easy, one of the first important tasks is to plan the transition process from the current state of diversity to the desired state. The transition process involves three distinct phases: (1) letting go of old ways, (2) a neutral zone when the old is gone but the new has not been fully operationalized, and (3) a new beginning (Bridges, 2003). Orchestrating an ending is as important as heralding a new beginning. The neutral zone represents the core of the transition process, as it is the period during which repatterning takes place (Bridges, 2003). Stakeholders can use the transition period to retool, learn, reflect, and change direction (Eisenhardt and Brown, 1999). As a result, speeding up the change process is not always the answer: finding the right rhythm can mean slowing down (Bridges, 2003). Time is needed for the absorption of change and for the reorchestration of organizational culture.

The terminology shown in Exhibit 1 helps to clarify avenues to inclusion and create the institutional bedrock of reciprocal empowerment. This lexicon of terms provides the theoretical underpinnings for institutionwide tactical planning. Twenty-first-century tactics must diagnose, neutralize, and overpower the more virulent, toxic forms of subtle, twenty-first-century discrimination.

Creating a Tactical Plan for Bridging the Diversity Divide

What core concepts can be used to create a tactical plan to implement the three-dimensional model of demography, diversity, and democracy? What specific approaches will ignite and sustain cultural change in support of diversity? How can prevailing frameworks of elitism and domination be dispelled?

EXHIBIT 1
New Lexicon for Bridging the Diversity Divide

Active Inertia   An organizational state characterized by four major markers: strategic frames or mindsets that become blinders; processes that harden into routines; relationships that become shackles limiting flexibility; and values that become dogmas (Sull, 2002). The point of active inertia is that this state is not simple passivity, but can be a chosen state for the organization.

Bias   An inflexible attitude or prejudgment about the character, abilities, or nature of an individual based on generalizations about the group to which the person belongs (Thiederman, 2003).

Cognitive Dissonance   The inconsistency between beliefs and behaviors that results in the individual's effort to resolve this disparity. When inconsistency is experienced, individuals feel frustrated and try to get rid of the source of their discomfort. For example, when individuals hold stereotypes, the tendency may be to reject information that is inconsistent with the stereotypes to eliminate cognitive dissonance.

Decategorization   The process by which group boundaries are deemphasized and individuals see themselves as separate individuals rather than members of separate groups (Gaertner and Dovidio, 2000). This process helps combats bias and complements the process of *recategorization*.

Defensive Avoidance   Behavior that involves information distortion and selective attention in situations that increase anxiety and fear (Huy, 1999).

Defensive Reasoning   A form of organizational defensiveness that has three major components: (1) individuals hold premises that may have questionable validity although they think otherwise; (2) they make inferences that do not follow from these premises although they believe they do; and (3) they reach conclusions they believe they have tested thoroughly yet they have not, as the way they have framed them renders them untestable (Argyris, 1990). The causes of defensive reasoning include the potential for embarrassment or threat (Argyris, 1990).

Diversity Backlash   Reaction to increasing diversity through heightened levels of discriminatory behavior (Yoder, 1991).

Emotional Balancing   A group-level process used in organizational development that juxtaposes emotion-related activities designed to drive change to induce continuity and enhance organizational adaptation (Huy, 2002).

Emotional Dissonance   Internal conflict between genuine emotions and those required to be displayed (Huy, 1999). The stronger a group's identity, the more intense the negative emotions that arise when change is proposed (Huy, 1999).

(Continued)

EXHIBIT 1 *(Continued)*

Emotional Intelligence   A class of intelligence that includes four branches: the ability to perceive emotion; use emotion to facilitate thought processes; analyze emotions and understand their outcomes; and manage emotion (Mayer, Salovey, and Caruso, 2004).

Emotionally Handicapped Organization   An organization in which individuals use their emotional intelligence to further self-interests and engage in emotional manipulation resulting in mistrust and cynicism at the organizational level (Huy, 1999). In contrast, the emotionally capable organization recognizes the interrelationship between emotion and change and institutionalizes practices that take emotions into account (Huy, 1999).

Organizational Intelligence   The ability of an organization to interpret and access information in a purposeful manner to increase its adaptive potential in the environment (Glynn, 1996). This concept implies that organizations that have more intelligent members as well as the ability to diffuse knowledge and institutionalize knowledge through organizational systems are more intelligent (Glynn, 1996).

Prejudice   Unfavorable attitude toward another group that involves both negative feelings and beliefs (Gaertner and Dovidio, 2000). Recent literature focuses on the nature of prejudice in terms of affective biases as contrasted with stereotyping or cognitive biases (Dipboye and Colella, 2005).

Punctuated Change   A theory of revolutionary organizational change that juxtaposes periods of relatively long-term incremental change to occasional dramatic revolutions or "reorientations" during which the organization sets its bearings for the next phase of change, overcomes inertia, and realigns strategy, power, and controls (Tushman and Romanelli, 1985, cited in Sastry, 1997). This form of change describes revolutionary periods of change that *punctuate* the change effort.

Recategorization   A process that encourages members of ingroups and outgroups to consider themselves as belonging to a common group that includes both memberships (Gaertner and Dovidio, 2000).

Reculturing   The transformational process of changing what is valued in a culture and the ways that individuals work to accomplish it (Fullan, 2002).

Scripts   Ritualistic approaches to conversation or behavior that replicate themselves without the interference of thought (Robbins, 2007; Tannen, 1994). Organizations have scripts such as "we have always done it that way before" as if the variables never change (Robbins, 2007).

(Continued)

EXHIBIT 1 *(Continued)*

Sense Making   The reconceptualization of the mental models and frameworks that will make sense of the diversity change and situate it in the context of existing organizational culture (Kezar and Eckel, 2002).

Slow Knowing   The tortoise-like slowness needed to absorb the complexity of change and elicit new patterns rather than a hare-brained chase after innovation (Claxton, 1997, cited in Fullan, 2001).

Stereotype   A cognitive schema that categorizes individuals, influences how information about the group is processed and recalled, and reflects unjustified beliefs about a group as a result of overgeneralization, unusual rigidity, and rationalization for prejudicial attitudes (Dovidio and Hebl, 2005). Individuals not fitting a stereotype are viewed as exceptions (Dovidio and Hebl, 2005). Stereotypes may encompass both affective (emotional) and cognitive responses and are highly resistant to change (Dovidio and Hebl, 2005).

Unintentional Intolerance   The use of stereotypes to brand people that are hardwired into a person's consciousness, difficult to erase, and may even be messages the individual would want to erase (Robbins, 2007). Even though the individual or group may not intend to exclude others, these preexisting messages get in the way.

The key concepts identified in the lexicon shown in Exhibit 1 provide logistical guidance in diversity implementation planning. These concepts focus on the *organizational-level* aspects of a major cultural change initiative. They also demonstrate the intricate interrelationship between individual behaviors and institutional change processes. This section summarizes some of the salient ideas that will help advance the tactical course of change captured in the lexicon. Further, the terminology offers deeper insight into the emotional aspects of change and highlights how organizations can adopt defensive postures and routines, remain actively inert, and still be emotionally handicapped. The concepts of emotional and cognitive dissonance reveal inconsistencies between internal attitudes and external behavior. Diagnosing these organizational and individual attributes in relation to diversity change will assist educational leaders as they consider approaches to inclusion.

Viewed from thirty thousand feet, organizations *mediate* the impact of large-scale social processes on organizational functioning (Ely and Thomas, 2001). In other words, the institutional stance toward diversity directly affects how diversity is valued in workplace contexts and processes. Despite the presence of lofty mission statements, if the organization is neutral or unsupportive toward diversity, substantive change is unlikely to occur. Furthermore, organizational theory suggests that organizations, like individuals, possess psychological attributes: they can reside in a state of active inertia, perpetuate defensive routines, lack *emotional intelligence,* or even be *emotionally handicapped* in terms of the inability to overcome the collective affective responses that impede the acceptance of diversity. Pain, change, and reparations are part of the organizational change process (J. R. Feagin, personal communication, January 6, 2006).

The concept of *unintentional intolerance* reveals how socially generated stereotypes or scripts unconsciously affect how minorities and women are viewed through the lens of the dominant culture (Robbins, 2007). Because of the presence of stereotypes and preconceptions, *cognitive dissonances* arise when new information is presented that conflicts with existing scripts (Robbins, 2007). Such dissonances are most easily resolved by simply rejecting or discrediting the contradictions (Robbins, 2007).

Dislodging pervasive stereotypes and scripts involves the difficult and arduous work of *reculturing* (changing what is valued in a culture) (Fullan, 2002). Merely hiring minorities and female faculty and staff will not address these deeper realities caused by the racial stratification that fosters inequality (Brown and others, 2003). The approach taken over the past three decades of simply bringing African Americans, Asian Americans, and Latino Americans into institutions that have remained static in culture is obviously inadequate (Brown and others, 2003).

Reculturing must address both cognitive and affective aspects of how diversity is viewed through the process of *cognitive sense making* and *emotional balancing.* Because transition involves the process of letting the old go, this process must not only make sense of the new but also address the emotional aspects of change. Emerging research on the cognitive and affective components of race bias shed light on the need to address both cognitive and emotional elements in the process of cultural change. Some research suggests that cognitive (stereotyping schemas) and affective (prejudicial attitudes) aspects of race bias may be conceptually independent (Amodio and Devine, 2006). Other research finds that prejudice and stereotyping are closely related and involve both affective and cognitive responses (Dovidio and Hebl, 2005). Despite these differing interpretations, most behaviors involve a network of brain regions and "there is not a single correspondence between a behavior and a brain structure" (Phelps and Thomas, 2003, p. 755). As a result, cognition, motivation, and affective responses cannot be separated "in any tidy fashion," and all must be considered in interventions design to promote ethical behavior (Fiske, 2004, p. 125). From this perspective, institutional initiatives need to balance emotional learning with cognitive components to address the deep-seated, culturally determined responses that permeate institutional culture.

The diffusion of *organizational intelligence* related to diversity across the boundaries of institutional subcultures is a slow and sometimes painful process. The concept of *slow knowing* refers to the need to allow sufficient time to absorb change and reduce the potential for diversity backlash (Fullan, 2002). The faster that leadership attempts to force change, the greater the tendency for shock waves of resistance to coalesce, forming a massive barrier impeding success (Black and Gregersen, 2002). A tactical plan for twenty-first-century organizational learning must first diagnose mental models of prejudice and bias and then identify how these models can be changed and displaced over time.

The next section introduces specific research-based approaches that will assist the university in its efforts to actualize reciprocal empowerment and overcome existing barriers to diversity. These approaches are designed to align practices, attitudes, and behaviors with institutional values, reinforce organizational learning in terms of diversity, stimulate the formation and growth of new mental models, and promote heightened engagement.

Research-Based Tactics That Promote Reciprocal Empowerment

The research-based approaches identified in this section offer concrete ways to overcome the barriers identified through the lexicon. As a tactical basis for implementing reciprocal empowerment, these action-oriented strategies address short-term objectives that foster long-term cultural change. We focus these strategies around the research findings on organizational change and group them in terms of how they draw on recent theory to operationalize empowerment. We offer nine suggested approaches based on the insights gained from the lexicon that address ways of overcoming stereotypes, addressing emotional balancing, supporting contributors to diversity initiatives, and building institutional safeguards.

Create Formal Programs That Enhance Intergroup Contact and Dispel Stereotypes

Institutional approaches are needed that balance affective and cognitive responses to diversity and reduce prejudice and stereotyping. Formal programs in which majority and minority group members collaborate and work toward common goals are important avenues to reducing "unintentional tolerance" and dispelling stereotypes. Research shows that intergroup bias between ingroups and outgroups is reduced by the creation of a *common identity* or a "superordinate" ingroup identity (Gaertner and Dovidio, 2000, p. 152). Furthermore, the reduction of bias occurs when these groups retain the notion of pluralism rather than assimilation (Gaertner and Dovidio, 2000). The crucial factor in establishing contacts that reduce prejudice is the *perceived importance* or instrumentality of the contact in helping individuals reach a valued goal (van Dick and others, 2004). As a result, structured institutional programs that emphasize commonality in purpose rather than competitiveness among groups and foster the attainment of valued goals for participants facilitate the attainment of reciprocal empowerment.

Research findings also demonstrate that recategorization of others and subsequent friendlier interpersonal relations result from the formation of racially mixed teams working toward a common goal, as direct interaction has been shown to reduce levels of intergroup bias (Gaertner and Dovidio, 2000). A comprehensive research study that examined 515 individual studies with 713 independent samples and 1,383 nonindependent tests validated the thesis advanced by Allport (1954) in *The Nature of Prejudice* that *direct contact* with *outgroups* reduces prejudice (Pettigrew and Tropp, 2006). Conscious efforts by university administrators to establish racially mixed committees tasked with significant goals can contribute to the reduction of existing biases. Such diverse work teams serve to heighten cooperation among members, as shown by a study of 138 graduate and undergraduate students in a large public university. Ethnically diverse teams that included Asians, blacks, and Hispanics performed more cooperatively than all-Anglo groups (Cox, Lobel, and McLeod, 1991).

As noted earlier, the stage of diversity an organization has reached mediates work group contexts. In monolithic organizations, categorization and stereotyping may predominate in work group settings (Larkey, 1996). By contrast in multicultural organizations, the tendency toward individuation or the ability to view the uniqueness of each person's characteristics may be reflected in work group contexts (Larkey, 1996). Research findings from a study conducted with 258 MBA students found that an organization's cultural emphasis influences the social categorization process (Chatman, Polzer, Barsade, and Neale, 1998). In this study, the creativity of diverse work groups was increased through access to a larger set of innovative ideas coupled with the team's belief that the ideas would work toward the benefit of the collective group (Chatman, Polzer, Barsade, and Neale, 1998). These findings demonstrate that the benefits of demographic diversity are more likely attained in organizations where the culture of the organization encourages people to view each other as working toward common purposes rather than when the culture emphasizes individualism (Chatman, Polzer, Barsade, and Neale, 1998).

On a microlevel, the perspective of a particular work group on diversity also directly affects power relations with respect to diversity and how the work group functions (Ely and Thomas, 2001). A study of three small firms that had already attained their affirmative action goals found that when a diverse work team views the cultural differences of its members as a significant resource for determining how best to accomplish core objectives and processes, such groups foster more symmetrical power relations and operate more efficiently (Ely and Thomas, 2001). In contrast, when work groups view cultural differences as having a marginal or even negative impact, the dominant group will be likely to define expectations about work through power relations (Ely and Thomas, 2001).

Practical application of these research findings requires organizational attentiveness to the composition and oversight of task forces, standing and ad hoc committees, screening and search committees, and work teams. The process of charging committees provides a valuable opportunity to share institutional values and to emphasize collaborative approaches and common goals. Structured organizational learning initiatives can incorporate the model for intergroup dialogue developed at the University of Michigan that involves consciousness raising, relationship building across differences, and enhancing both individual and collective abilities to promote social justice (Zúñiga, Nagda, Chesler, and Cytron-Walker, 2007).

As a note of caution, however, institutional support that creates conditions of competition or unequal status can in fact increase animosity between groups, diminishing the effect of intergroup contact (Pettigrew and Tropp, 2006). Reducing intergroup anxiety that leads to feelings of threat and uncertainty needs to be considered in programmatic efforts to reduce prejudice through increased contact (Pettigrew and Tropp, 2006).

A real question that arises in this regard is whether affirmative action programs increase intergroup competitiveness and give rise to negative feelings toward outgroups. A study of 231 minority faculty members of the American Psychological Association indicates that when affirmative action programs are perceived as nonvoluntary and imposed, these faculty members experienced a less positive departmental climate and also experienced greater self-doubt which undermined job satisfaction (Niemann and Dovidio, 2005). By contrast, when such programs are seen as voluntary in terms of sincere and willing departmental efforts to recruit minorities and females in support of institutional affirmative action policies, minority faculty experienced a more positive departmental climate and also experienced less self-doubt (Niemann and Dovidio, 2005). These results suggest that both institutional and departmental leadership are critical in articulating the larger benefits of affirmative action for the entire organization to mitigate the effects of intergroup competition. Politicizing diversity so that one side must win and the other must lose detracts from the ability of institutions to build programs that *complement* the existing affirmative action framework (R. R. Thomas, 2006).

Build an Institutional Safety Net for Those Who Have Traditionally Been Marginalized

Research has shown the effects of oppressive dynamics on individuals and how hegemonic internalization results in personal blame and lowered self-esteem

(Prilleltensky and Gonick, 1996). Support groups that provide safe zones for dialogue facilitated by professionals from areas such as counseling or social psychology can help counteract the impact of unfavorable biases and provide coping mechanisms (Evans and Chun, 2008). Such groups provide the opportunity for development of problem-focused and emotion-focused coping strategies. Problem-focused strategies aim at restructuring the situation to reduce the opportunity for marginalization, while emotion-focused strategies address controlling the emotions so as not to escalate situations (Crocker and Major, 1989; Evans and Chun, 2007b; Kuo, 1995).

Ensure That Organizational Safeguards Mediate the Organizational Impact of Demographic Differences in Supervisory and Peer-to-Peer Relationships

When assessing climate and diversity outcomes, little systematic institutional attention has been given to the impact of demographic differences in supervisory and peer-to-peer relations. Minorities and women in general have less access to key supervisory roles. For example, a research study with 727 respondents in U.S. work establishments found a large gender gap in women in supervisory roles across virtually all specifications (Huffman, 1995). Demographic differences in supervisory relationships may influence the outcome of formal organizational processes such as performance evaluation and promotion and tenure. Lack of support in the workplace is one of the most pervasive informal barriers for minorities and women (Evans and Chun, 2007a). Subtle patterns of differing expectations and standards, exclusion from promotional pipelines and decision-making processes, and isolation or tokenism can impede the success of women and minorities (Evans and Chun, 2007a).

Building a climate of support that sensitizes supervisors to differing perceptions of fairness held by subordinates is a significant factor in job satisfaction and retention (Wesolowski and Mossholder, 1997). For example, a study conducted at two service firms with 296 participants found that the racial composition of supervisor-subordinate dyads affected perceptions of procedural justice and job satisfaction of subordinates (Wesolowski and Mossholder, 1997).

Development of supervisory skills that allow more empathetic relationships with demographically diverse subordinates is an urgently needed focus in workforce training (Wesolowski and Mossholder, 1997). Because minority and female faculty and staff often experience lack of supervisory support as a major barrier, the institution benefits from attentiveness to the subtle signals that reflect the marginalization of minorities and women in certain departments or subcultures.

Identification of recurring patterns of problems in specific departments that reflect demographic differences between supervisor and subordinate requires careful analysis and sustained review. Furthermore, to create welcoming departments, department chairs and administrators need to be conscious of the impact of institutionalized racism as well as the racial and gender composition of their departments and the impact on minority newcomers (Bensimon, Ward, and Sanders, 2000).

Create Structural Processes That Recognize and Reward Diversity Contributions

Establishing reward programs for diversity contributions fosters reciprocity between the faculty and staff and the university. In this regard, a positive correlation has been found between employees' affiliation with the organization and higher levels of innovation when reward strategies are implemented (Eisenberger, Fasolo, and Davis-LaMastro, 1990). Organizational reciprocity occurs when individuals desire to contribute to an organization because of the encouragement provided through explicit institutional recognition of the emotion-based aspects of organizational commitment (Eisenberger, Fasolo, and Davis-LaMastro, 1990). This recognition in turn fosters a sense of unity and shared values between the employee and the organization (Eisenberger, Fasolo, and Davis-LaMastro, 1990). Diversity reward strategies must reinforce the alignment of individual and organizational values, promote psychological empowerment, and convey institutional support.

A prominent example of faculty reward strategies that explicitly recognize diversity contributions is the newly revised promotion and tenure process for the University of California system. The report of the president's task force on faculty diversity signed by the chancellors of the eleven campuses asks each campus to examine resource allocation and incentives, including allocation of full-time positions in light of a newly revised systemwide policy that recognizes research, teaching, and service promoting diversity in the consideration of tenure and promotion (University of California, 2006). The revised promotion and tenure policy includes language related to diversity contributions: "Teaching, research, professional, and public service contributions that promote diversity and equal opportunity are to be encouraged and given recognition in the evaluation of the candidate's qualifications. These contributions to diversity and equal opportunity can take a variety of forms, including efforts to advance equitable access to education, public service that addresses the needs of California's diverse population, or research in a scholar's area of expertise that highlights inequalities" (University of California, Los Angeles, 2005, p. 4).

The establishment of a blue-ribbon commission on diversity at the University of Colorado under the leadership of a new system president represents a bold approach to diversity practices (Brown, 2005). The commission comprises forty civic, corporate, and education leaders reporting to the system president and charged with providing external review of diversity programs on the Boulder, Colorado Springs, and Denver campuses (Brown, 2005). As a result of the commission's work, the Colorado Springs campus proposed new diversity reward strategies that include recommendations to reward diversity in the hiring, merit review, and tenure processes for faculty (Shockley-Zalabak, 2006). These strategies include evaluating departmental diversity when awarding tenure and tenure-track positions to departments; reviewing departmental tenure criteria to incorporate credit for diversity in research, teaching, and service; ranking requests for new positions based on diversity of past hiring pools; recognizing diversity service in faculty merit reviews; and making additional compensation available for faculty who serve on recruiting committees and in mentoring programs (Shockley-Zalabak, 2006).

Model Reciprocal Empowerment Through Mentorship

Mentorship is a vehicle for giving power to others through a mutually beneficial process that models reciprocal empowerment. In this regard, social capital theory emphases the significance of resources in an individual's social networks that benefit the success of actions (Lin, 2001). Traditionally, the inequality of social capital has resulted in fewer opportunities for women and minorities to mobilize resources and promote their careers (Lin, 2001). Mentoring enhances the social capital of mentees and can serve as a bridge to different social circles that may have significant resource differentials (Lin, 2001). The act of mentoring can also help effect personal transformation of the mentor and rejuvenate mentors' careers through greater fulfillment and increased confidence (Ehrich, Hansford, and Tennent, 2004; Girves, Zepeda, and Gwathmey, 2005).

The value of mentoring programs to minority and female scholars has received increasing attention in recent higher education literature (see for example Bensimon, Ward, and Sanders, 2000; Niemann and Dovidio, 2005; Ragins, 1995; Turner, Myers, Samuel, and Creswell, 1999). Department chairs play an instrumental role as mentors in guiding new faculty in teaching, research, and institutional citizenship related to successful attainment of tenure (Bensimon, Ward, and Sanders, 2000). Chairs can also use their position to protect minority academics from "cultural taxation" and being overused by their department in diversity activities because of their own sense of obligation (Bensimon, Ward, and Sanders, 2000). Mentoring opens channels to minorities and women that can prevent career derailment, reduce isolation, nurture self-confidence, alleviate self-doubt, and improve job satisfaction in the academic workplace (Niemann and Dovidio, 2005; Turner, Myers, Samuel, and Creswell, 1999). Formalization of mentoring programs through regularized funding sources, communication of the importance of these programs, and creation of opportunities for cross-racial contact are tactical approaches that strengthen the value of mentoring in promoting reciprocal empowerment.

Mentoring relationships can be purely instrumental in nature and focused on career development or can foster a true mentor-protégé relationship that provides psychosocial support in terms of affirmation, maintenance of self-esteem, and professional identity (Thomas, 1993). A study of twenty-two cross-racial mentoring relationships between white and African American employees found that relationships were less likely to progress from instrumental to mentor-protégé relationships when the parties did not share a common strategy for dealing with racial difference—either discussing it openly or suppressing and denying it (Thomas, 1993). Effective networks for minorities may benefit from instrumental relationships with white sponsors without relying on these sponsors exclusively for psychosocial support (Ibarra, 1995).

Establish Accountability Measures to Monitor Progress in Meeting Diversity Goals

As stewards of public funds, public research universities bear responsibility to ensure accountability in the delivery of education, research, and workplace policies and practices. In this regard, public research universities hold a special mandate to respond to the most urgent cultural, economic, and policy issues of their region and the nation (University of Toronto, 2006). Requiring accountability for diversity progress is a tactical approach that helps drive the attainment of actual results. A number of institutional diversity plans have identified the importance of accountability to measure progress in meeting diversity goals.

For example, the North Carolina State University diversity plan, "Inclusive Excellence" (2007b), which paired accountability with recognition for diversity, represents one of seven strategic diversity goals. Accountability measures include requiring that all unit leaders contribute toward progress in diversity; ensuring that each employee's job description, work plan, and evaluation support a diverse work environment; and increasing the number of job offers that articulate support for diversity as a condition of employment (North Carolina State University, 2007a). Similarly, the strategic plan at the University of Vermont (2007) identifies the need to create a diverse community as its first goal and identifies nine performance indicators to monitor progress and ensure accountability for this goal.

Build Synergy for the Diversity Initiative by Blending Top-Down Leadership with Grassroots Leadership and Support in Campus Subcultures

Effective change needs to engage stakeholders from different campus subcultures throughout the process of developing diversity plans. In addition, each organizational unit needs to be allowed to finds its own path to the new organization, as forcing change from the top only short-circuits change (Beer, Eisenstat, and Spector, 1990). Because universities can be understood as cultural systems, diversity leaders must understand the lived experiences of the campus, interpret their themes, and decipher their symbolic processes and shared meanings (Bensimon, 1990).

An example of how a lack of grassroots support can derail administrative efforts was the vocal faculty opposition generated in response to a draft five-year diversity plan at the University of Oregon in 2005. The university had to scale back the plan because of the criticism it generated from two dozen professors (Gose, 2006). A controversial aspect of the plan was the inclusion of assessment of the cultural competency of professors as part of the tenure and posttenure review process (Gose, 2006). The plan also called for hiring forty faculty members by 2012 to teach courses in a cluster of diversity-related topics, which some viewed as too costly (Silverman, 2005). The following year, President Dave Frohnmayer issued a new plan requiring that each college, school, and unit develop its own strategic action plan, which the university senate adopted (University of Oregon, n.d.). The new plan resulted in the creation of a strategic action plan by every unit in the college (Frohnmayer, 2008). While recognizing the diversity of opinion in relation to approaches to equity and the deep contention that had accompanied the plan's development, President Frohnmayer concluded that the entire process had yielded common ground and shared commitment (2008). As one commentator noted, perhaps the plan had moved too quickly and not taken the time to build support through relationships and attempting smaller goals first (Gose, 2006).

Based on the Example of the Civil Rights Movement, Incorporate the Leadership of Majority Group Members to Spearhead Diversity Efforts

This tactical approach is a concrete example of reciprocal empowerment and draws on lessons learned from the civil rights movement in which white civil rights leaders played instrumental roles leading to the success of the movement. For example, Jack Greenberg, civil rights attorney, headed the NAACP's Legal Defense and Educational Fund for thirty-five years and achieved some of the civil rights movement's most significant legal victories such as *Brown* v. *Board of Education* [347 U.S. 483 (1954)], *Griggs* v. *Duke Power Co.* [401 U.S. 424 (1971)], and *Coker* v. *Georgia* [433 U.S. 584 (1977)] (Feldman, 1996). Other whites who made substantial contributions to the civil rights movement include Morris Dees of the Southern Poverty Law Center and Ralph Neas of the Leadership Conference on Civil Rights (Feldman, 1996).

When only minorities are involved in diversity initiatives, such efforts can be perceived as merely residing in areas of organizational culture that have limited social capital or are undervalued (Aguirre and Martinez, 2006). Engaging the leadership of majority group members facilitates the recognition needed for successful action. This approach recognizes the value of a broader constituency rather than narrow representation. In this regard, Wise (2008b) serves as an eloquent spokesperson against racism and "institutionalized white supremacy" (p. xi). From the vantage point of a majority group member, he has even greater ability than members of minority groups to challenge what he terms "willed ignorance," to uncover truth, and to engage in a courageous critique of the practices and advantages of racial privilege (p. xi).

Spark Organizational Learning Initiatives Using Experiential Means That Address Emotional and Affective Responses to Diversity

Transformation of institutional culture requires more than the occasional obligatory diversity speaker or lecture. When increased organizational rhetoric centers around diversity, even greater backlash or resistance to change may develop. This reaction to diversity operates like a form of reverse psychology. Focusing attention on diversity may have the opposite effect. Many forms of diversity training can simply increase resistance and create even further polarization. Training that assumes a didactic approach may be the *least* effective means of changing minds and creating new mind-sets.

Instead, the road to deepened understanding of diversity requires exposure to different pathways and approaches. One major pathway is knowledge based in terms of discussion of sociohistorical frameworks, the nature of contemporary forms of discrimination, and awareness of concepts such as unintentional tolerance. Another major pathway is experiential such as through the medium of improvisational theater. Interactive theater provides a powerful channel to illuminate cognitive dissonances with respect to diversity and to engage participants on a deeper emotional and experiential level. Such interactions that address racism, heterosexism, sexism, ageism, or classism foster experiential learning that may have a greater effect than lectures or other forms of rational information processing in terms of changing attitudes and behaviors (Tromski and Doston, 2003).

At the University of Nebraska–Lincoln, for example, a program of diversity education for students incorporating artistic expression and guest speakers heightened the ability of the participants to empathize with experiences of discrimination and inequality (Kubal, Meyler, Stone, and Mauney, 2003). An improvisational theater group formed at Temple University by the director of learning and development in human resources facilitates conversations about similarities and differences through improvisations and allows actors to say and do things that others may not be able to do (Watson, 2008). Behavioral and organizational barriers to diversity can be depicted in the medium of improvisational theater to build recognition of the subtleties of twenty-first-century discrimination. Portraying the roles of protagonists, assistants, bystanders, and dissenters to racial events can promote a more nuanced understanding of how discrimination occurs within work contexts (Picca and Feagin, 2007).

Concluding Observations

Transformational change occurs in periods of "punctuated equilibrium" that require sufficient time for transition and the absorption of change. The best strategies do more than simply take an organization from Point A to Point B and balance the need for transition with the introduction of structural change that promotes diversity. The emotional aspects of change must be taken into account, as individuals exhibit signs of grieving that accompany organizational shifts (Bridges, 2003). Orchestrating change means accommodating the slow release of prior expectations, norms, assumptions, and behaviors and replacing them gradually with new models and patterns.

In the context of decentralized academic cultures, as the experiences at the University of Oregon demonstrate, readiness and grassroots support are essential. Without sufficient preparation or support, the chief diversity officer or leaders charged with implementing diversity can experience institutional backlash driven by the intensity of institutional politics and entrenched factions (Williams and Wade-Golden, 2007b).

Although review of current workplace practices reveals the emergence of a number of comprehensive diversity strategic plans, the real test remains whether or not diversity programs result in perceptible change in behaviors, processes, and outcomes. Is the culture more welcoming to minorities and women? Does accountability involve any significant consequences when goals are not met? Are rewards based on demonstrated contributions to diversity progress? In the effort to attain tangible progress, we introduce representative tools and practices in the next chapter that will assist the university in the transformational change needed to attain reciprocal empowerment.

A Toolkit for Operationalizing Reciprocal Empowerment

> Leadership, then, is not mobilizing others to solve problems we already know how to solve, but to help them confront problems that have never yet been successfully addressed.
>
> [Fullan, 2001, p. 3]

DIVERSITY PLANNING REQUIRES CONCRETE TOOLS, policies, and approaches that will advance organizational learning and shift the cultural frame to inclusive power relations and a core ideology of reciprocal empowerment. The genesis of such planning derives from organizational will and commitment to diversity. The real work for institutional leadership then lies in reculturing in complex situations—a process that cannot be captured in checklists (Fullan, 2001). As a result, the focus of this chapter is on representative tools that will begin the evolutionary process of "slow knowing" and cultural transformation in support of diversity. Adaptation and amplification of these tools to specific subcultures and institutional purposes enhance their effectiveness and applicability.

From an organizational standpoint, reculturing needs to uncover and address institutional dysfunctions that hinder the attainment of diversity. The five dysfunctions of a team identified by Lencioni (2002)—absence of trust, fear of conflict, lack of commitment, avoidance of accountability, and inattention to results—can be applied to organizational barriers that impede diversity progress. Without resolving underlying conflicts, covert and overt resistance to diversity obstructs cultural change.

As we explore specific tools that promote institutional reculturing, we first discuss how formal, externally driven pressures can assist in the process. The accreditation process and institutional effectiveness planning provide such opportunities. A sample matrix links optimal cultural traits for diversity with institutional effectiveness. We then turn to organizational learning approaches that will begin the difficult conversations needed to surface and resolve internal conflicts related to diversity. Specific tools and approaches are suggested that create nonthreatening organizational learning interventions.

External Measures of Internal Progress: Accreditation and Diversity

One of the most widely accepted formal drivers of change in academic institutions is the accreditation process. Accreditation represents a powerful external impetus that provides the opportunity to review mission and ensure its congruity with institutional goals. The outcomes-based orientation of accreditation review buttressed by a culture of evidence provides a natural medium for charting and ensuring diversity progress. Through a process of peer review, external pressures emanating from accreditation heighten the importance and visibility given to continuous improvement. As a result, accreditation provides a significant opportunity for examining the effectiveness of organizational processes that support diversity and inclusion.

Given the delicate balance in recent Supreme Court decisions related to diversity, diversity guidelines by accrediting agencies can perhaps best be framed in terms of social policy (Finkin, 1994). For these reasons, the Statement on Diversity approved in 1994 by the Western Association of Schools and Colleges is framed as a policy guideline that does not have the force and effect of accreditation standards but instead represents expected areas of good practice (Western Association of Schools and Colleges, 2001). As such, the statement provides the most significant example of an accreditation policy that explicitly links expectations for institutional review to diversity.

The association's Statement on Diversity emphasizes the need for a climate of respect for diverse backgrounds, ideas, and perspectives as well as campus engagement on issues of diversity. Five key elements are identified in terms of expectations for institutional review:

Examination of institutional mission and purpose in light of diversity;

Achievement of representational diversity among students, faculty, administrative staffs, and governing boards based on the institution's own view of its constituency and mission;

Appreciation of diversity as an outcome of undergraduate instruction;

A cocurricular environment that fosters the development of all students;

Strengthened efforts to make diversity integral to plans for institutional improvement (Western Association of Schools and Colleges, 2001).

The asssociation's diversity statement further articulates the relationship between diversity and educational quality. It defines diversity as *prospective* in its effort to create an environment that supports the aspirations of all members of the campus community, compared with the retrospective view of affirmative action (Western Association of Schools and Colleges, 2001). The statement also highlights the value of collegiality in encouraging debate and evaluating competing ideas (Western Association of Schools and Colleges, 2001).

All six regional accrediting agencies identify *institutional integrity* as an important standard and value, and two (the New England and Western associations) link institutional integrity to diversity. All similarly identify the role of mission and goals as central to accreditation. The most comprehensive link between institutional integrity and diversity is made by the Western Association in terms of the need to respond to social demographic trends in policies, cocurricular programs, and administrative practices.

Not all stakeholders view accreditation as an appropriate vehicle for monitoring progress in diversity. For example, a study of 160 institutions in 1996 that included 81 public institutions found that 56.8 percent of the respondents did not support the use of regional accreditation to promote diversity among the faculty (Ezeamii, 1996). The race of the survey respondent, correlated with the predominant race of the student body, significantly affected this view: more whites than expected disagreed about the value of accreditation in promoting faculty diversity, and more nonwhites agreed (Ezeamii, 1996).

Yet despite this perspective, faculty diversity remains a clear theme in a number of the accreditation standards. The passage of time has made it clear that dramatic trends in globalization coupled with changing student demographics have permanently altered the landscape for diversity in public research universities.

Given the recent Supreme Court decisions on admissions, language relating to diversity standards in accreditation processes has undergone increased scrutiny. For example, in 2007 the National Advisory Committee on Institutional Quality and Integrity that advises the Department of Education challenged the American Bar Association's revision of its diversity standards. It limited the association's authority to eighteen months instead of five years for several reasons, including its changes to the diversity standards. The bar association had extended the existing diversity standard beyond students to faculty and staff and reframed admissions criteria that referred to "victims of discrimination" to reference underrepresented groups, in particular racial and ethnic minorities (Pekow, 2006). The standard also called on law schools to offer opportunities to members of minority groups, whereas the former standard had referenced "qualified members" (Pekow, 2006). Later, the legal counsel for the Department of Education stated that it would appeal the national advisory committee's decision to let the diversity standards remain in place (Mangan, 2007).

Even in this changing judicial climate, the University of California at Los Angeles issued an institutional proposal to the Western Association of Schools and Colleges (2006) that provides a clear example of how diversity can be approached in the accreditation process. The proposal identifies six distinctive and interrelated hallmarks consistent with the role of a public research university, one of which is diversity. On this pressing issue, the report cites progress in faculty diversity, organizational structures, student diversity, and curricular diversity.

Consistent with the evolving view of diversity as social policy, common themes that support an institution's progress toward diversity and inclusion in regional accreditation standards include responsiveness to the increasing diversity in society; institution-specific diversity goals; valuing people; collaboration;

involvement; respect for diversity and human dignity; equity and justice; equitable and consistent treatment of all constituencies in appointment, evaluation, and promotion; and adherence to legal requirements. These themes represent significant leverage points that allow an institution to review its internal processes, structures, and climate in relation to the realization of equity, justice, and reciprocal empowerment. Despite the narrowing definitional window of how diversity goals can be articulated, accreditation presents a very real opportunity for comparative and ongoing study of organizational outcomes in light of the institution's diversity vision.

Institutional Effectiveness and Diversity Progress

Another important vehicle for driving change through formal institutional processes is to link diversity progress with the attainment of institutional effectiveness. The concept of institutional effectiveness is integral to outcomes assessment. In particular, the Southern Association of Colleges and Schools (SACS) considers institutional effectiveness one of the most important elements in reaccreditation. The Accrediting Council for Independent Colleges and Schools also provides guidelines and standards for planning, evaluation, and assessment of institutional effectiveness (2004). Institutional effectiveness gauges whether an institution achieves what it says it does. This research-based approach requires ongoing systematic review and evaluation.

Specific and credible arguments for cultural change need to provide insight into how inclusion will enhance institutional effectiveness. *Reframing* the issue of diversity in terms of educational mission and the need to sustain the integrity of the academic disciplines assists with the difficult process of implementing cognitive insights that can instigate cultural change (Smith, 1995).

As public research universities compete for scarce resources in an era of budgetary constraints and institute performance measures to gauge progress, attainment of diversity-related outcomes can serve as a significant differentiator in terms of institutional effectiveness. Diversity has proven to be a catalyst for institutional improvement, as shown by the progress made by forty

FIGURE 4
Theoretical Model of Culture Traits

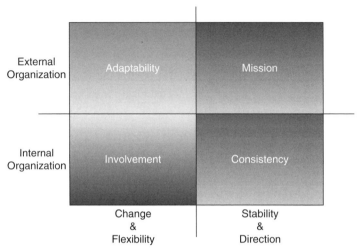

Source: Denison and Mishra, 1995, p. 216.

institutions that received Lilly grants between 1991 and 1994 (Musil and others, 1999).

The relationship between workplace culture and organizational effectiveness has received increasing attention in the research literature. For example, a study of the culture of five large organizations identified specific cultural traits that have an impact on effectiveness (Denison and Mishra, 1995). These traits, shown in Figure 4, balance change and stability as well as internal integration and external adaptation (Denison and Mishra, 1995). In tandem with these findings, general dimensions of organizational culture noted in the research literature focus on a number of key themes that include the basis of truth and rationality, orientation and focus, isolation versus collaboration, accountability and responsibility, time horizon, orientation to work and others, innovation and personal growth (Detert, Schroeder, and Mauriel, 2000).

Based on the principles in Denison and Mishra's model (1995), a matrix for gauging the relationship of diversity to institutional effectiveness can serve as the impetus for discussion in terms of five institutional levers that will bridge the diversity divide: organizational learning, policies, reward and recognition, leadership and accountability, and structures and resources (see Exhibit 2).

EXHIBIT 2
Linking Culture and Effectiveness: Five Levers for Bridging the Diversity Divide

Linking Culture and Effectiveness	Thematic Principles	Organizational Learning/ Development	Policies	Reward and Recognition	Leadership and Accountability	Structures and Resources
Adaptability	Inclusive excellence; globalization; innovation; agility; community	How do organizational development programs address demographic diversity and globalization?	How do policies reference diverse perspectives and a diverse workforce?	How do formal organizational processes provide explicit recognition for contributions to diversity goals?	Has leadership discussed inclusive excellence or a similar concept?	Does the institution have a designated diversity officer with budget and resources?
Involvement	Reciprocal empowerment; inclusion; collaboration; motivation; orientation to others	Are administrators and supervisors trained on coaching, mentoring, and empowerment?	How do policies reference inclusiveness?	Are inclusion, collaboration, and empowerment recognized in evaluation processes?	Is leadership evaluated on attainments in empowerment or inclusion?	Does the institution devote resources to educating the workforce on inclusion?
Consistency	Orientation and focus; truth and rationality; inclusion and equity	What organizational development programs address equity?	How do policies address equity in human resource processes?	How does the institution recognize attainment of equity goals?	How is long-term progress in attaining equity measured?	What structures and budgetary resources are devoted to equity?
Mission	Diversity and reciprocal empowerment	How do organizational development programs address the relation of mission and diversity?	How do policies address the interrelationship of diversity and mission?	How do institutional recognition programs link diversity and mission?	What leadership goals pertain to diversity outcomes and mission?	Does the budget support alignment of diversity and mission?

Internal Change: Organizational Learning Tools for Cultural Transformation

Because the preeminent challenge of organizational learning is to create new mind-sets, this section offers representative approaches that can foster greater alignment between individuals and the institution's core diversity values, generate meaningful dialogue, and transform mind-sets. Controversy and conflict will inevitably surface as tectonic shifts in the cultural landscape occur and forces of resistance emerge. Yet the framework of demography, diversity, and democracy is an institutional reference point that crystallizes aspirations and connects the university with the global community. We offer concrete suggestions about how to operationalize organizational learning through formal statements and organizational development interventions.

Create a Diversity Manifesto

As a starting point for strengthening alignment with mission and values in the culture, a diversity manifesto is an internal branding tool that will help solidify the change effort. A diversity manifesto will not only coalesce the key principles of a commitment to diversity but also provide a thematic guideline for practices, policies, and conduct. As such, it creates a powerful impetus for cultural and behavioral change. To be successful, however, the process of creating a manifesto cannot be driven from the top down; it needs to involve key constituencies and ensure grassroots support from all subcultures in the academic institution.

For example, the principles of community developed at the University of California, Davis have served as a successful manifesto on community that emphasizes service to society through a climate of justice, respect for the dignity of all, support for diverse perspectives, and nondiscrimination (2003). Adopted in 1990, the principles of community were written over eighteen months, with input from a wide variety of campus constituencies, including the academic senate, students, and staff. The principles provide a broad yet concrete framework of universitywide expectations for conduct, interaction, climate, and freedom of expression. As such, the principles create clear obligations for the members of a diverse university community to contribute to a climate of support and respect. It is not an isolated statement, as policies and resources are linked to its execution and implementation. Given its explicit expectations linked to climate and conduct, a diversity manifesto creates an environment conducive to the realization of reciprocal empowerment.

Create Nonthreatening Organizational Learning Interventions

Because of the potential for diversity training to backfire and ignite a diversity backlash, nonthreatening organizational learning interventions based on sound research principles will begin the conversations needed for change. The word "conversation" derives from the Latin *convertere,* which means "turning together" and implies a partnership that leads to true dialogue (based on the Greek *dialogos* or "flow of meaning") (Senge and others, 2008).

Yet while a significant body of research exists on organizational learning, relatively few practical tool sets exist that specifically apply to diversity in the higher education environment. Appendix B lists some of the most relevant and applicable resources for organizational development for diversity in the higher education workplace.

One of the most useful research-based analyses that demonstrates how to create the institutional conversations needed for organizational learning is a study that draws on research results from four hundred companies in forty counties (Yeung, Ulrich, Nason, and Von Glinow, 1999). This study yielded the following simple formula for how organizations learn: Learning Capability = Generating Ideas × Generalizing Ideas with Impact (Yeung, Ulrich, Nason, and Von Glinow, 1999). By extension in the research university environment, this formula means that generalizing the value of diversity must take place across all institutional sectors and subcultures.

The attainment of learning capability, however, can be blocked by seven specific organizational learning disabilities that apply also to the area of diversity:

Environmental blindness—the inability to perceive gaps between actual and desired organizational states;

Simplemindedness—the absence of formal methods for analyzing and responding to opportunities or threats;

Homogeneity—the failure to include differing sources, voices, and perspectives;

Tight coupling—the lack of flexibility and adaptability in a tightly controlled institutional setting;

Paralysis—the inability to implement new procedures or take action;

Superstitious learning—the inability to interpret experiences accurately as a result of using limited data, faculty assumptions, or irrational myths;

Diffusion deficiency—the failure to diffuse ideas throughout the organization as a result of the dynamics of power or the rigidity of political structures (Yeung, Ulrich, Nason, and Von Glinow, 1999).

As an instrument for discussion about organizational diversity disabilities, the group exercise shown in Exhibit 3 can be used to generate discussion about the institution as a whole:

Other organizational development interventions can be developed to identify core organizational defensive routines. The Left-Hand/Right-Hand Case

EXHIBIT 3
Auditing Diversity Disabilities

On a 10-point scale, please honestly assess the extent to which your organization suffers each of the following learning disabilities:

Diversity Disabilities	Current Level as of Today	Required Level for Future Success	Areas for Improvement
Environmental Blindness			
Simplemindedness			
Homogeneity			
Tight Coupling			
Paralysis			
Superstitious Learning			
Diffusion Deficiency			
Average Score			

Source: Modified from Yeung, Ulrich, Nason, and Von Glinow, 1999, p. 166.

Method (Argyris, 2004), which can be applied to diversity organizational defensive routines, asks participants to do the following:

1. Describe a key organizational problem in one paragraph from your perspective.

2. Assuming you could talk to anyone you wished to solve the problem, describe in one paragraph the strategy you would use in the meeting.

3. Divide the page into two columns, and write in the left-hand column what you did or would say. In the right-hand column, write what you believe the other individual would say. Write your response to their response. Continue for two typewritten pages or so.

4. In the left-hand column, write any idea or feeling you would not communicate for any reason.

This exercise can be used in large groups from one institution or from multiple institutions to educate participants about the power and widespread existence of organizational defensive routines (Argyris, 2004). It also enables the participants to begin to redesign their actions as they analyze the theories in use (Argyris, 2004).

A more specific organizational learning intervention can be designed to bring majority group males into greater realization of their role in building multicultural coalitions (see Exhibit 4). This concept has great relevance to higher education because of the potential for institutionalizing multicultural coalitions (Crowfoot and Chesler, 1996). As a point of departure, the types of incentives lending support for white males' participation in social justice work based on Crowfoot and Chesler's work (1996) are summarized in Exhibit 4 as a starting point for discussion.

In efforts to support majority male participation in diversity initiatives, both incentives and accountability mechanisms can assist in moving majority individuals from status quo to transformative responses. Incentivizing tactics such as recognition awards and opportunities for intergroup contact as well as experientially and affectively-based diversity training assist in this movement. The articulation of a strong "business case" for diversity provides a clear institutional rationale for diversity. Accountability measures such as clearly focused

EXHIBIT 4

Incentives to Participate in Diversity and Social Justice Work for Majority Males

Nature of Incentive	Status Quo Response	Transformative Responses
Advance common good	Incremental change without changing power structure	Redistribute resources and power
Help others	Paternalistic help	Reciprocal empowerment
Self-growth (meet unmet group needs)	Deal with "special" minorities and women as exceptions without a fundamental change in attitude	Reduce privilege, make amends for hurtful behavior
Self-interest (enhance own group)	Selective sensitivity while maintaining dominating behaviors	Equitable sharing and collaborative approaches

Source: Based on Crowfoot and Chesler, 1996.

position descriptions and specific diversity goals will also be needed, however, to help provide the impetus for change.

In addition, as institutions seek to develop core working groups that will help turn the tide in support of diversity and inclusion, the concept of growing a strategic microcosm of change provides a valuable organizational learning model for instigating more widespread efforts (Senge and others, 2008). A series of guided questions will help those involved to develop a disciplined approach to expanding the network with a view to creating a tipping point for organizational change (Senge and others, 2008):

What key players have not yet been included in the network? Why? Have institutional walls played a part in the fact that they have not yet been included?

Are there key players that we may not see because they are hidden in the institution's blind spots? Who can help identify actors who have been overlooked?

When is the appropriate time to reach out to those not part of the current circle? How can those who are currently excluded be engaged in the strategic microcosm?

The representative tools in this section are based on the most current organizational development research and can help generate meaningful and honest dialogue about diversity impediments in the institutional landscape. These tools provide concrete ways to elicit discussion about why cultural change in support of diversity and reciprocal empowerment are both valuable to institutional success and urgent in terms of the global imperative to maintain competitiveness and maximize talent.

Concluding Observations

A persuasive mandate for diversity is needed to change institutional culture. Without such a mandate, diversity will remain little more than window dressing or occasional rhetoric. The mandate must crystallize and convey clear organizational will and commitment: political power must accompany the will to transform the organization. This power can emanate from the board of trustees, the president, governance structures, unions, faculty, students, and diverse constituencies internal and external to the university. Although senior leadership is vital and indispensable in efforts to integrate diversity in the academy, the dynamism to fuel organizational change comes from other levels of the organization that may be closer to the pulse of a campus (Anderson, 2007).

For example, in 2006 the Black Student Union at Indiana University–Purdue University at Indianapolis threatened to file a lawsuit unless university officials addressed several areas of concern, including the creation of a black student center, an undergraduate degree curriculum for African American studies, and a budget of $78,000 for black student organizations (Indiana University–Purdue University at Indianapolis, 2006). The university's chancellor held a series of open forums with students, faculty, and staff and laid out steps the university planned to take, including the formation of a multicultural center, a full-time campus diversity officer, and a cultural competency program for university employees (Powers, 2006). This example demonstrates how the power of the student constituency provided the impetus for diversity change.

Even the most effective organizational learning tools have no appreciable impact without an unwavering commitment from institutional leadership to attain results. In contrast, a persuasive mandate for diversity framed in the model of demography, diversity, and democracy enables the institution to engage stakeholders, build an expansive network, and mobilize the systems and resources needed to stay the course through prolonged, sustained efforts. This type of sustained effort is in general antithetical to university culture that often prefers quick solutions and immediate results.

Effective leadership also needs to address the emotional tension that surrounds diversity by telling the truth and acknowledging the reality of negative emotions (Senge and others, 2008). Over some period of time, the emotional tension around diversity characterized by fear, anxiety, and distrust can be supplanted by creative tension directed toward changing reality through sustained efforts (Senge and others, 2008). Overcoming distrust is a major hurdle on the pathway to a fully functional organization. Unresolved intergroup conflicts undermine democratic participation and thwart the potential for social justice and stability (Zúñiga, Nagda, Chesler, and Cytron-Walker, 2007).

A change model built on research-based organizational development principles facilitates and accelerates the success of institutionwide diversity initiatives. Given the complexity of the higher education environment, such a model will provide a sense of how change will unfold, what variables must be considered, and ways to overcome resistance. Although change is not linear (Fullan, 2001), it can develop from seemingly microcosmic efforts multiplied exponentially. As institutions purposefully eliminate residual sources of dysfunctionality and vault each successive hurdle on the journey to inclusion, these progressive efforts will create the momentum needed for cultural transformation.

Reprise: Recommendations and Implications

WITH THE ADVENT OF GLOBALIZATION, the rise of the knowledge economy, and rapid global and local changes in demography, institutional transformation in support of diversity and inclusion has become an urgent strategic imperative. Denial of the need for inclusion is a myopic approach: an institutional blindness that can be compared with simply freezing in one's tracks as the distance between the world as it is and the world as one wants it to be becomes too great (Tedlow, 2008). Institutions of higher education are now at the threshold of a new universe in which talent overshadows and obscures the historic divides of race, ethnicity, gender, disability, and other manifestations of difference.

Despite these accelerating trends, universities have been slow to embrace and implement a purposeful and deliberate approach to diversity and empowerment in the workplace. As leaders in the creation of knowledge, research universities face the challenge of creating high-commitment, high-performance organizations (Eisenstat and others, 2008). In an era of increasing competition and scarce resources, this challenge demands the realization of the full capabilities of a diverse workforce and an inclusive approach to talent acquisition and retention.

Findings from the corporate sector reveal key factors in the attainment of high-commitment, high-performance organizations that illustrate how reciprocal empowerment can facilitate organizational success. A research study of twenty-two chief executive officers of organizations in Europe and America finds that leaders of high-commitment, high-performance organizations combine four strategies: they earn the trust of their organizations, they are deeply engaged with their employees, they have a focused agenda, and they devote substantive efforts to building the organization's collective leadership (Eisenstat and others, 2008). Each of these four strategies requires reciprocal empowerment—trust, engagement, a common agenda, and collective-leadership.

Yet when leaders take employees' commitment for granted, they risk the destruction of the social fabric of their organizations (Eisenstat and others, 2008). High-performance organizations recognize that the work environment requires openness, flexibility, and interdependence that will only develop in a psychologically safe environment, especially when faced with changing or complex situations (Edmondson, 2008). An unbalanced focus on employee accountability without psychological safety can result in organizational dysfunctions that hinder performance (Edmondson, 2008). Reciprocal empowerment frees the organization of a culture of fear because it honors the democratic principles of inclusion, participation, and self-definition.

A recent survey of great colleges to work for that included fifteen thousand respondents at eighty-nine institutions of higher education explored the components of an exceptional work environment (Selingo, 2008). The survey confirmed a significant disconnect between senior administrators and employees. Faculty members at public institutions indicated less confidence in senior leadership than their private counterparts (56 percent versus 65 percent) (Selingo, 2008). The survey also showed that over the course of employees' careers, typically after eight years in a campus job and as employees hit their late forties, career satisfaction diminishes in terms of career development, fairness, and job satisfaction (Selingo, 2008). This study validates the role of senior leadership in the creation of an empowering and inclusive workplace characterized by fairness and opportunities for growth and development.

The model of demography, diversity, and democracy melds contemporary global realities with American moral and ethical values. It provides a foundational model for a workplace that has overcome dysfunctional internal conflict surrounding diversity. Internal conflict constrains institutional progress and diminishes external competitiveness. As universities recognize the relation of inclusive excellence to institutional success, this recognition will enhance the progressive attainment of a workplace that celebrates the talent, innovation, and creativity of all its members.

Throughout the monograph, we have argued for the importance of organizational learning as a powerful channel for institutional transformation in support of diversity. When institutions simply focus on getting things done and getting them done as efficiently as possible without taking time for reflection, experimentation, and learning, people do not have enough time to learn, critical information does not reach the top, and unhealthy internal competition arises (Edmondson, 2008). Rather than execution-as-efficiency, the concept of execution-as-learning promotes sustainable success—as organizations focus on learning faster rather than getting things done more efficiently (Edmondson, 2008). Key steps in supporting organizational learning for diversity include making it safe to learn, institutionalizing disciplined reflection, providing tools for collaboration, establishing process guidelines, and collecting process data (Edmondson, 2008).

A new paradigm for diversity shifts from a focus on structural representation to a learning-and-effectiveness model that connects diversity to approaches to work (Thomas and Ely, 1996). This approach allows the institution to incorporate employees' perspectives into the principal work of the organization and to rethink strategies, missions, tasks, practices, and cultures (Thomas and Ely, 1996).

Because culture change in support of diversity is one of the most difficult problems universities face today, a research-based model for the change process will help avoid false starts, reduce time delays, and provide ways to overcome inevitable resistance. An organizational diversity success model creates the diversity vision, builds organizational commitment, ensures a capable workforce, and is reinforced on an ongoing basis (Chang, 1996).

From review of the literature and research presented in this monograph, we offer the following recommendations for operationalizing reciprocal empowerment in the workplace:

Develop a change model for diversity based on research-based organizational
   learning principles;
Formally articulate the framework of diversity principles and values that
   underpin the change process in collaboration with campus constituencies;

Enhance organizational learning capacity for diversity and reciprocal empowerment through resource allocation, state-of-the-art programs, and supportive infrastructure;

Develop bench strength in human resources for a comprehensive talent management strategy;

Embark on a process of careful assessment to determine the extent to which the workplace culture supports diversity and reciprocal empowerment;

Ensure that the organization has safety valves such as an employee assistance program, formal mediation and counseling programs, listening programs, and support groups that allow women and minority faculty and staff to develop coping approaches to difficult workplace challenges;

Monitor retention of minorities and women and be alert to issues of disparate treatment, especially patterns of subtle, everyday discrimination;

Emphasize and codify civility and respect as critical to a compassionate organization;

Create psychologically safe modes of engagement on issues of diversity that dispel stereotypes and strengthen commonality of purpose;

Showcase success stories of reciprocal empowerment that transcend differences.

In his prophetic essay "World House" based on his Nobel Peace Prize lecture, Dr. Martin Luther King, Jr. (1967), recognized the impact of scientific and technological revolutions that have created a "worldwide neighborhood" and noted that we are at a turning point in history as "oppressed people cannot remain oppressed forever" (King, 1967, para. 8). He called for a "true revolution of values" led by America and noted the need to bridge the gulf between scientific progress and moral progress (King, 1967, para. 5). His "Letter from a Birmingham Jail" of April 16, 1963, summarizes these themes most eloquently: "Injustice anywhere is a threat to justice everywhere. We are caught in an inescapable network of mutuality, tied in a single garment of destiny. Whatever affects one directly, affects all indirectly" (King, 1963, para. 4).

Exclusion and marginalization of women and minorities in the higher education workplace are costly, as they seal the institution off from the sources of knowledge, creativity, and innovation that lead to vitality and success. Leaders who perpetuate white privilege and power are one dimensional in that they limit their own knowledge and access to the cultural riches that can save humanity from future problems and disasters (Feagin, forthcoming).

In contrast, when an institution of higher education actively seeks to create a workplace of respect, such efforts yield significant benefits to all stakeholders: faculty and staff, students, the campus community, and society at large. As an exemplar of a diverse democracy and a leader in the revolution of values, the public research university offers the promise of bridging the diversity divide through a true network of mutuality and reciprocal empowerment that values and celebrates the talents of all its members.

Appendix A
Sample Matrix for Gauging Gaps in Diversity Leadership

Multidimensional Reference	Goals	Outcomes	Measures/Data Collection Mechanisms	Baseline	Bench-marks	Time Line
Demography	Increase representation of minorities and women at executive levels	Diverse leadership	Affirmative action and equity plan data			
Diversity	Ensure inclusion of diverse leadership in decision making	Collaboration, participation, and incorporation of multiple perspectives in decision making	Delegation of authority and responsibility; inclusive consultative processes; composition of decision-making bodies			
Diversity and Democracy	Mission statement refers to diversity as core value	Mission statement moves beyond structural representation to inclusion; identifies diversity strategic intent	Demonstrated links to resources, programs, and policies			
Democracy	Reciprocal empowerment of minorities and women	Resource sharing, promotional leadership opportunities, reward and recognition salary progression	Review of resource bases and scope of authority; comparative statistics on salaries, merit increases, and promotions disaggregated by race and gender			
Demography, Diversity, and Democracy	Diversity Strategic Plan	A results-oriented plan that addresses culture, climate, and reciprocal empowerment in the workplace				

Appendix B: Resource Guide

Representative Publications on Diversity Learning and Planning

Anderson, J. A. (2007). *Driving change through diversity and globalization: Transformative leadership in the academy.* Sterling, VA: Stylus.

This book provides a learning-centered framework for discussion about diversity. It offers a range of tools designed to shape academic dialogue and incorporate diversity as an integral aspect of the teaching and learning paradigm.

Clayton-Pedersen, A. R., and others. (2007). *Making a real difference with diversity: A guide to institutional change.* Washington, DC: Association of American Colleges and Universities.

This publication contains a carefully researched institutionalization rubric for evaluating campus progress in diversity work. The rubric provides an evaluation tool that measures five key elements in progress toward diversity: goals, capacity, leadership, resources, and centrality of diversity. The publication highlights findings from the James Irvine Foundation Campus Diversity Initiative (2000–2005) that was designed to assist twenty-eight higher education institutions in California in the improvement of campus diversity.

Lee, M. W. (2004). *The art of mindful facilitation.* Berkeley, CA: StirFry Seminars and Consulting.

As a practical field guide, this compendium contains specific diversity exercises and vignettes designed to foster greater understanding of diversity and to build community based on the principles of mindful facilitation.

Musil, C. M., and others. (1999). *To form a more perfect union: Campus diversity initiatives.* Washington, DC: Association of American Colleges and Universities.

This monograph is one in a series of three collaborative cross-institutional studies that summarize the lessons and insights gained by scholars in the implementation of diversity initiatives designed to promote academic excellence.

Williams, D. A., Berger, J. B., and McClendon, S. A. (2005). *Toward a model of inclusive excellence and change in postsecondary institutions.* Washington, DC: Association of American Colleges and Universities.

Commissioned as part of the Making Excellence Inclusive initiative of the Association of American Colleges and Universities, this paper examines the dimensions of organizational behavior most relevant to inclusive excellence and presents an inclusive excellence change model that integrates these dimensions. Of special interest is the Inclusive Excellence Scorecard that can be used as a comprehensive assessment framework for evaluating diversity progress.

Yeung, A. K., Ulrich, D. O., Nason, S. W., and Von Glinow, M. A. (1999). *Organizational learning capability: Generating and generalizing ideas with impact.* Oxford, England: Oxford University Press.

As one of the few research-based resources that demonstrates how to stimulate organizational learning, this book provides a series of exercises that can be adapted for diversity work and will create the institutional dialogue needed for change.

Zúñiga, X., Nagda, B. A., Chesler, M., and Cytron-Walker, A. (2007). *Intergroup dialogue in higher education: Meaningful learning about social justice.* San Francisco: Jossey-Bass.

This resource provides concrete guidelines on how to implement sustained intergroup dialogue based on a model implemented at the University of Michigan. Although primarily designed for students, a variant of this type of design can be used for ongoing dialogue among faculty and staff.

Key Web Sites

American Association of University Professors, www.aaup.org/AAUP/issuesed/diversity/Diversitybib.htm

The American Association of University Professors Web site contains a bibliography on diversity compiled by the Committee on Historically Black Institutions and Scholars of Color.

American Council on Education, http://www.acenet.edu

The American Council on Education serves more than eighteen hundred institutions of higher education and provides programs and initiatives such as the ACE Fellows program that has prepared diverse and talented faculty and administrators for senior leadership roles. The Center for Advancement of Racial and Ethnic Equity (CAREE) publishes an annual status report entitled "Minorities in Higher Education" that provides in-depth statistical analysis of enrollment trends, awarding of degrees, and employment trends.

American Institute for Managing Diversity, Inc., http://aimd.org/index.php

The American Institute for Managing Diversity was founded by Roosevelt Thomas in 1984 and is a leading nonprofit think tank devoted to promoting the field of diversity management. Its Web site includes a wide variety of resources, including an annotated bibliography, articles, and information about diversity education conferences.

Association of American Colleges and Universities, http://www.aacu.org/resources/diversity/index.cfm

The Association of American Colleges and Universities serves more than eleven hundred institutions of higher education. Under the direction of Caryn McTighe Musil, senior vice president, Office of Diversity, Equity, and Global Initiatives, the Web site on diversity provides comprehensive resources, including AAC&U publications, diversity initiatives, conferences, and a wide variety of resources. The Web site also provides three research-based briefing papers that provide in-depth perspective on attaining inclusive excellence on campus.

CUPA-HR Knowledge Center, http://cupahr.org/knowledgecenter/index.asp

The College and University Professional Association for Human Resources Knowledge Center provides timely analyses, articles, and resources on key topics related to human resources in higher education.

National Association of Diversity Officers in Higher Education, http://www.nadohe.org/

The Web site of the National Association of Diversity Officers in Higher Education is a national forum for campuses and chief diversity officers and showcases best practices in diversity strategic planning in higher education.

Society for Human Resource Management, http://www.shrm.org/kc/

The Society of Human Resource Management's Knowledge Center provides a wide array of resources to its members, including a talent management toolkit, research reports and articles, benchmarking studies, and white papers on human resource topics.

References

Accrediting Council for Independent Colleges and Schools. (2004). *Institutional effectiveness: A guide to implementation.* Retrieved August 11, 2008, from http://www.acics.org/ Publications/ieg.asp.

Aguirre, A., Jr., and Martinez, R. O. (2006). Diversity leadership in higher education. *ASHE-ERIC Higher Education Report,* vol. 32, no. 3. San Francisco: Jossey-Bass.

Allen, K., Jacobson, S., and Lomotey, K. (1995). African American women in educational administration: The importance of mentors and sponsors. *Journal of Negro Education, 64*(4), 409–422.

Allport, G. (1954). *The nature of prejudice.* Cambridge, MA: Addison-Wesley.

American Association of University Professors. (2007). *Diversity bibliography.* Retrieved August 24, 2008, from www.aaup.org/AAUP/issuesed/diversity/Diversitybib.htm.

American Council on Education. (2008). Retrieved August 24, 2008, from http://www.acenet.edu.

American Institute for Managing Diversity, Inc. (n.d.). Retrieved August 24, 2008, from http://aimd.org/index.php.

Amodio, D. M., and Devine, P. G. (2006). Stereotyping and evaluation in implicit race bias: Evidence for independent constructs and unique effects on behavior. *Journal of Personality and Social Psychology, 91*(4), 652–661.

Anderson, J. A. (2007). *Driving change through diversity and globalization: Transformative leadership in the academy.* Sterling, VA: Stylus.

Argyris, C. (1990). *Overcoming organizational defenses: Facilitating organizational learning.* Boston: Allyn & Bacon.

Argyris, C. (1993). Education for leading-learning. *Organizational Dynamics, 21*(3), 4–7.

Argyris, C. (1997). Learning and teaching: A theory of action perspective. *Journal of Management Education, 21*(1), 9–26.

Argyris, C. (2004). *Reasons and rationalizations: The limits to organizational knowledge.* Oxford, England: Oxford University Press.

Argyris, C., and others. (1994). The future of workplace learning and performance. *Training and Development, 48*(5), 36–47.

Association of American Colleges and Universities. (2008). Retrieved August 24, 2008, from http://www.aacu.org/resources/diversity/index.cfm.

Association of American Colleges and Universities. (2009). *Making excellence inclusive.* Retrieved January 25, 2009, from www.aacu.org/inclusive_excellence/index.cfm.

Astin, A. W. (1991). *Assessment for excellence: The philosophy and practice of assessment and evaluation in higher education.* Santa Barbara, CA: American Council on Education/ Oryx Press.

Astin, A. W. (1993, March). Diversity and multiculturalism on the campus: How are students affected? *Change, 25,* 44–49.

Atkinson, R. C. (2001). *The globalization of the university.* Retrieved February 7, 2009, from http://www.rca.ucsd.edu/speeches/japanspc.htm.

Atkinson, R. C., and Pelfrey, P. A. (2006). Opportunity in a democratic society: Race and economic status in higher education. *Proceedings of the American Philosophical Society, 150*(2), 318–332.

Baker, R. L. (2002). Evaluating quality and effectiveness: Regional accreditation principles and practices. *Journal of Academic Librarianship, 28*(1/2), 3–7.

Barnett, R. (2005). Recapturing the universal in the university. *Educational Philosophy and Theory, 37*(6), 785–797.

Becker, B. E., Huselid, M. A., and Ulrich, D. (2001). *The HR scorecard: Linking people, strategy, and performance.* Boston: Harvard Business School Press.

Beer, M., Eisenstat, R. A., and Spector, B. (1990). Why change programs don't produce change. *Harvard Business Review, 68*(6), 158–166.

Bell, D. (1993). Foreword: The power of prophets. In B. W. Thompson and S. Tyagi (Eds.), *Beyond a dream deferred: Multicultural education and the politics of excellence* (pp. ix–x). Minneapolis: University of Minnesota Press.

Bell, L. A. (1997). Theoretical foundations for social justice education. In M. Adams, L. A. Bell, and P. Griffin (Eds.), *Teaching for diversity and social justice: A sourcebook* (pp. 3–15). New York: Routledge.

Bensimon, E. M. (1990). The new president and understanding the campus as a culture. In W. G. Tierney (Ed.), *Assessing academic climates and cultures* (pp. 75–95). San Francisco: Jossey-Bass.

Bensimon, E. M., Polkinghorne, D. E., Bauman, G. L., and Vallejo, E. (2004). Doing research that makes a difference. *Journal of Higher Education, 75*(1), 104–126.

Bensimon, E. M., Ward, K., and Sanders, K. (2000). *The department chair's role in developing new faculty into teachers and scholars.* Bolton, MA: Anker Publishing.

Bernal, D. D., and Villalpando, O. (2002). An apartheid of knowledge in academia: The struggle over the "legitimate" knowledge of faculty of color. *Equity and Excellence in Education, 35*(2), 169–180.

Birnbaum, R. (1992). *How academic leadership works: Understanding success and failure in the college presidency.* San Francisco: Jossey-Bass.

Black, J. S., and Gregersen, H. B. (2002). *Leading strategic change: Breaking through the brain barrier.* Upper Saddle River, NJ: Prentice Hall.

Board of Trustees. (2006). *Mission and purposes of the University of Connecticut.* Retrieved August 3, 2007, from http://policy.uconn.edu/pages/findPolicy.cfm?PolicyID=194.

Bonilla-Silva, E. (2003). *Racism without racists: Color-blind racism and the persistence of racial inequality in the United States.* Lanham, MD: Rowman & Littlefield.

Bonilla-Silva, E. (2006). *Racism without racists: Color-blind racism and the persistence of racial inequality in the United States* (2nd ed.). Lanham, MD: Rowman & Littlefield.

Bonner, F. A., II. (2006). The temple of my unfamiliar. In C. A. Stanley (Ed.), *Faculty of color: Teaching in predominantly white colleges and universities* (pp. 80–99). Bolton, MA: Anker Publishing.

Bowen, W. G., Bok, D., and Burkhart, G. (1999). A report card on diversity: Lessons for business from higher education. *Harvard Business Review, 77*(1), 138–149.

Brase, W. C. (2005). *Sustainable performance improvement.* Retrieved August 2, 2008, from http://www.abs.uci.edu/media/RevisedSustainablePerformanceImprovement.pdf.

Brase, W. (n.d.). *Why some enterprise improvement models are more effective than others.* Retrieved August 2, 2008, from http://net.educause.edu/ir/library/pdf/ffp0008s.pdf.

Brayboy, B.M.J. (2003). The implementation of diversity in predominantly white colleges and universities. *Journal of Black Studies, 34*(1), 72–86.

Bridges, B. K., Eckel, P. D., Cordova, D. I., and White, B. P. (2008). *Broadening the leadership spectrum: Advancing diversity in the American college presidency.* Washington, DC: American Council on Education.

Bridges, W. (1994). *JobShift: How to prosper in a workplace without jobs.* Reading, MA: Addison-Wesley.

Bridges, W. (2003). *Managing transitions: Making the most of change* (2nd ed.). Cambridge, MA: Perseus.

Brockbank, W. (1999). If HR were really strategically proactive: Present and future directions in HR's contribution to competitive advantage. *Human Resource Management, 38*(4), 337–352.

Brockbank, W., Ulrich, D., and Beatty, R. W. (1999). HR professional development: Creating the future creators at the University of Michigan Business School. *Human Resource Management, 38*(2), 111–117.

Brown, A. D., and Starkey, K. (2000). Organizational identity and learning: A psychodynamic perspective. *Academy of Management Review, 25*(1), 102–120.

Brown, C. L. (1998). Campus diversity: Presidents as leaders. *College Student Affairs Journal, 18*(1), 84–93.

Brown, H. (2005). *President Brown's invitation to participate.* Retrieved September 24, 2007, from https://www.cu.edu/diversity/brc/invite.html.

Brown, M. K., and others. (2003). *Whitewashing race: The myth of a color-blind society.* Berkeley: University of California Press.

Burud, S. L., and Tumolo, M. (2004). Leveraging the new human capital: Adaptive strategies, results achieved, and stories of transformation. Palo Alto, CA: Davies-Black.

Campus climate reports. (2002). Bibliography. Retrieved August 31, 2007, from http://www.lgbtcampus.org/resources/campus_climate.html.

Bridging the Diversity Divide

CBS News. (2008, March 18). *Transcript: Barack Obama's speech on race.* Retrieved March 23, 2008, from http://www.cbsnews.com/stories/2008/03/18/politics/main3947908_ page2.shtml.

Chait, R., Holland, T. P., and Taylor, B. E. (1993). *The effective board of trustees.* Phoenix: Oryx Press.

Chait, R., Holland, T. P., and Taylor, B. E. (1996). *Improving the performance of governing boards.* Phoenix: Oryx Press.

Chang, M. J. (n.d.). *Who benefits from racial diversity in higher education?* Retrieved June 9, 2007, from http://www.diversityweb.org/Digest/W97/research.html.

Chang, R. Y. (1996). *Capitalizing on workplace diversity.* San Francisco: Jossey-Bass.

Chatman, J. A., Polzer, J. T., Barsade, S. G., and Neale, M. A. (1998). Being different yet feeling similar: The influence of demographic composition and organizational culture on work processes and outcomes. *Administrative Science Quarterly, 43*(4), 749–780.

Chew, C. M. (2008). Deconstructing the politics of race. *Diverse: Issues in Higher Education, 25*(5), 9.

Chronicle of Higher Education. (2007). *Forum: What can be done to diversify executive suites? 54*(5), B48. Retrieved October 7, 2007, from http://chronicle.com/weekly/v54/i05/05b04801.htm.

Chun, E. (2004, May). *Sample diversity scorecard.* Paper presented at the meeting of the College & University Professional Association for Human Resources, Newport, RI.

Claxton, G. (1999). *Hare brain tortoise mind: How intelligence increases when you think less.* United Kingdom: Fourth Estate.

Clayton-Pedersen, A., and Musil, C. M. (2005). *Introduction to the series.* Retrieved May 15, 2006, from http://www.aacu.org/inclusive_excellence/documents/Williams_et_ al.pdf.

Clayton-Pedersen, A. R., and others. (2007). *Making a real difference with diversity: A guide to institutional change.* Washington, DC: Association of American Colleges and Universities.

Collaborative on Academic Careers in Higher Education. (2007). *The one-two policy punch: Be sure to consider importance and effectiveness.* Retrieved August 25, 2007, from http://gseacademic.harvard.edu /~coache /reports/20070801.html.

College and University Professional Association for Human Resources Knowledge Center. (2008). Retrieved August 24, 2008, from http://cupahr.org/knowledgecenter/index.asp.

Collins, J. C. (2001). *Good to great: Why some companies make the leap—and others don't.* New York: HarperBusiness.

Cooper, J., and Stevens, D. D. (Eds.). (2002). *Tenure in the sacred grove: Issues and strategies for women and minority faculty.* Albany: State University of New York Press.

Cox, T., Jr. (2001). *Creating the multicultural organization: A strategy for capturing the power of diversity.* San Francisco: Jossey-Bass.

Cox, T. H., Lobel, S. A., and McLeod, P. L. (1991). Effects of ethnic group cultural differences on cooperative and competitive behavior on a group task. *Academy of Management Journal, 34*(4), 827–847.

Crenshaw, K., Gotanda, N., Peller, G., and Thomas, K. (1996). Introduction. In K. Crenshaw, N. Gotanda, G. Peller, and K. Thomas (Eds.), *Critical race theory: The key writings that formed the movement* (pp. xiii–xxxii). New York: New Press.

Crocker, J., and Major, B. (1989). Social stigma and self-esteem: The self-protective properties of stigma. *Psychological Review, 96*(4), 608–630.

Crosby, F. J. (2004). Affirmative action is dead: Long live affirmative action. New Haven, CT: Yale University Press.

Crowfoot, J. E., and Chesler, M. A. (1996). White men's roles in multicultural coalitions. In B. P. Bowser and R. G. Hunt (Eds.), *Impacts of racism on white Americans* (2nd ed., pp. 202–229). Thousand Oaks, CA: Sage.

Cruz, D. M. (1995). Struggling with the labels that mark my ethnic identity. In R. V. Padilla and R. C. Chávez (Eds.), *The leaning ivory tower: Latino professors in American universities* (pp. 91–100). Albany: State University of New York Press.

Cudd, A. E. (2006). *Analyzing oppression.* New York: Oxford University Press.

Darlington, P. S. E., and Mulvaney, B. M. (2003). *Women, power and ethnicity: Working toward reciprocal empowerment.* Binghamton, NY: Haworth Press.

Deitch, E. A., and others. (2003). Subtle yet significant: The existence and impact of everyday racial discrimination in the workplace. *Human Relations, 56*(11), 1299–1324.

Delgado, R., and Stefancic, J. (2001). *Critical race theory: An introduction.* New York: NYU Press.

Denison, D. R., and Mishra, A. K. (1995). Toward a theory of organizational culture and effectiveness. *Organization Science, 6*(2), 204–223.

Detert, J. R., Schroeder, R. G., and Mauriel, J. J. (2000). A framework for linking culture and improvement initiatives in organizations. *Academy of Management Review, 25*(4), 850–863.

Dipboye, R. L., and Colella, A. (2005). An introduction. In R. L. Dipboye and A. Colella (Eds.), *Discrimination at work: The psychological and organizational bases* (pp. 1–10). Mahwah, NJ: Erlbaum.

Dovidio, J. F., and Hebl, M. R. (2005). Discrimination at the level of the individual: Cognitive and affective factors. In R. L. Dipboye and A. Colella (Eds.), *Discrimination at work: The psychological and organizational bases* (pp. 11–36). Mahwah, NJ: Erlbaum.

Drucker, P. F. (1985). *Innovation and entrepreneurship: Practice and principles.* New York: HarperBusiness.

Easterby-Smith, M., Crossan, M., and Nicolini, D. (2000). Organizational learning: Debates past, present and future. *Journal of Management Studies, 37*(6), 783–796.

Eastern Washington University. (2002). Proposal to the board of trustees for an EWU diversity initiative. Retrieved August 7, 2008, from http://www.ewu.edu/groups/diversity/FinalProposal.pdf.

Eastern Washington University. (2008). EWU board of trustees diversity initiative. Retrieved August 7, 2008, from http://www.ewu.edu/x1904.xml.

Edmondson, A. C. (2008). The competitive imperative of learning. *Harvard Business Review, 86*(7/8), 60–67.

Ehrich, L. C., Hansford, B., and Tennent, L. (2004). Formal mentoring programs in education and other professions: A review of the literature. *Educational Administration Quarterly, 40*(4), 518–540.

Eisenberger, R., Fasolo, P., and Davis-LaMastro, V. (1990). Perceived organizational support and employee diligence, commitment, and innovation. *Journal of Applied Psychology*, 75(1), 51–59.

Eisenhardt, K. M., and Brown, S. L. (1999). Time pacing: Competing in markets that won't stand still. In *Harvard business review on managing uncertainty* (pp. 175–202). Boston: Harvard Business School Press.

Eisenstat, R. A., and others. (2008). The uncompromising leader. *Harvard Business Review*, 86(7/8), 50–57.

Ely, R. J., and Thomas, D. A. (2001). Cultural diversity at work: The effects of diversity perspectives on work group processes and outcomes. *Administrative Science Quarterly*, 46(2), 229–273.

Evans, A., and Chun, E. B. (2007a). Are the walls really down? Behavioral and organizational barriers to faculty and staff diversity. *ASHE-ERIC Higher Education Report*, vol. 33, no. 1. San Francisco: Jossey-Bass.

Evans, A., and Chun, E. B. (2007b). Coping with behavioral and organizational barriers to diversity in the workplace. *CUPA-HR Journal*, 58(1), 12–18.

Evans, A., and Chun, E. B. (2008). Closing the chasm of subtle second generation discrimination. *CUPA-HR Journal*, 59(2), 2–9.

Ezeamii, H. C. (1996, October). *Faculty diversity and regional accreditation: Crucial issues and a survey of academic leaders.* Paper presented at an annual meeting of the Association for the Study of Higher Education, Memphis, TN.

Fain, P. (2005). Surveys find governing boards are older and slightly more diverse. *Chronicle of Higher Education*, 51(43), A21. Retrieved August 13, 2008, from http://chronicle.com/weekly/v51/i43/43a02101.htm.

Farrell, E. F., and Van Der Werf, M. (2007). Playing the rankings game. *Chronicle of Higher Education*, 53(38), A11–A19.

Feagin, J. R. (2006). *Systemic racism: A theory of oppression.* New York: Routledge.

Feagin, J. R. (forthcoming). *The white racial frame.* New York: Routledge.

Feagin, J. R., and O'Brien, E. (2003). *White men on race: Power, privilege, and the shaping of cultural consciousness.* Boston: Beacon Press.

Feagin, J. R., and Vera, H. (2001). *Liberation sociology.* Boulder, CO: Westview Press.

Feagin, J. R., Vera, H., and Imani, N. (1996). *The agony of education: Black students at white colleges and universities.* London: Routledge.

Fegley, S. (2006, January). *2006 talent management survey report.* Retrieved January 1, 2008, from http://www.shrm.org/hrresources/surveys_published/2006%20Talent%20Management%20Survey%20Report.pdf.

Feldman, J. (1996). Race-consciousness versus colorblindness in the selection of civil rights leaders: Reflections upon Jack Greenberg's crusaders in the courts. *California Law Review*, 84(1), 151–166.

Fenelon, J. (2003). Race, research, and tenure: Institutional credibility and the incorporation of African, Latino, and American Indian faculty. *Journal of Black Studies*, 34(1), 87–100.

Finkin, M. W. (1994). The unfolding tendency in the federal relationship to private accreditation in higher education. *Law and Contemporary Problems, 57*(4), 89–120.

Firebaugh, F. M., and Miller, J. R. (2000). Diversity and globalization: Challenges, opportunities, and promise. *Journal of Family and Consumer Sciences, 92*(1), 27–36.

Fiske, S. T. (2004). Intent and ordinary bias: Unintended thought and social motivation create casual prejudice. *Social Justice Research, 17*(2), 117–127.

Fletcher, M. A., and Cohen, J. (2009, January 19). Far fewer consider racism big problem: Little change, however, at local level. *Washington Post*, p. A6.

Florida, R. (2002a). The economic geography of talent. *Annals of the Association of American Geographers, 92*(4), 743–755.

Florida, R. (2002b). *The rise of the creative class: And how it's transforming work, leisure, community and everyday life.* New York: Basic Books.

Florida, R. (2006). Regions and universities together can foster a creative economy. *Chronicle of Higher Education, 53*(4), B6. Retrieved May 10, 2007, from http://chronicle.com/weekly/v53 /i04/04b00601.htm.

Florida, R. (2007). *The flight of the creative class: The new global competition for talent.* New York: Collins.

Florida, R., and Goodnight, J. (2005). Managing for creativity. *Harvard Business Review, 83*(7–8), 124–131.

Foley, J., with Kendrick, J. (2006). *Balanced brand: How to balance the stakeholder forces that can make or break your business.* San Francisco: Jossey-Bass.

Ford, R. T. (2005). *Racial culture: A critique.* Princeton, NJ: Princeton University Press.

Freire, P. (Ed.). (1989). *Pedagogy of the oppressed.* New York: Continuum.

Friedman, T. L. (1999). *The Lexus and the olive tree.* New York: Farrar, Straus, Giroux.

Friedman, T. L. (2005, April 3). It's a flat world, after all. *New York Times Magazine, 154*(53173), 32–37.

Frohnmayer, D. (2008). President's spring 2008 letter. Retrieved April 19, 2008, from http://president.uoregon.edu/ news/springletter.shtml.

Fullan, M. (2001). *Leading in a culture of change.* San Francisco: Jossey-Bass.

Fullan, M. (2002). The change leader. *Educational Leadership, 59*(8), 16–20.

Fullan, M. (2008). *The six secrets of change: What the best leaders do to help their organizations survive and thrive.* San Francisco: Jossey-Bass.

Fullan, M. G. (1994). *Coordinating top-down and bottom-up strategies for educational reform.* Retrieved March 5, 2009 from http://www.ed.gov/pubs/EDReformStudies/SusReforms/fullan1.html.

Gaertner, S. L., and Dovidio, J. F. (2000). *Reducing intergroup bias: The common ingroup identity model.* Philadelphia: Psychology Press.

Gappa, J. M., Austin, A. E., and Trice, A. G. (2007). *Rethinking faculty work: Higher education's strategic imperative.* San Francisco: Jossey-Bass.

Garcia, M., and others. (2001). *Assessing campus diversity initiatives: A guide for campus practitioners.* Washington, DC: Association of American Colleges and Universities.

Girves, J. E., Zepeda, Y., and Gwathmey, J. K. (2005). Mentoring in a post–affirmative action world. *Journal of Social Issues, 61*(3), 449–479.

Glynn, M. A. (1996). Innovative genius: A framework for relating individual and organizational intelligences to innovation. *Academy of Management Review, 21*(4), 1081–1111.

Gonzalez, M. C. (1995). In search of the voice I always had. In R. V. Padilla and R. C. Chávez (Eds.), *The leaning ivory tower: Latino professors in American universities* (pp. 77–90). Albany: State University of New York Press.

Gose, B. (2006). The rise of the chief diversity officer. *Chronicle of Higher Education, 53*(6), B1. Retrieved April 18, 2008, from http://chronicle.com/free/v53/i06/06b00101.htm.

Graham, S. (2006). *Diversity: Leaders not labels.* New York: Free Press.

Grossman, R. J. (2007). New competencies for HR. *HRMagazine, 52*(6), 58–62.

Hamel, G., and Prahalad, C. K. (1989). Strategic intent. *Harvard Business Review, 67*(3), 63–78.

Hamilton, N. W. (2004). Faculty involvement in system-wide governance. In W. G. Tierney (Ed.), *Competing conceptions of academic governance: Negotiating the perfect storm* (pp. 77–103). Baltimore: Johns Hopkins University Press.

Hansen, H. K., and Salskov-Iversen, D. (2005). Remodeling the transnational political realm: Partnerships, best-practice schemes, and the digitalization of governance. *Alternatives, 30*(2), 141–164.

Hardiman, R., and Jackson, B. W. (1997). Conceptual foundation for social justice courses. In M. Adams, L. A. Bell, and P. Griffin (Eds.), *Teaching for diversity and social justice: A sourcebook* (pp. 16–29). New York: Routledge.

Harris, C. I. (1996). Whiteness as property. In K. Crenshaw, N. Gotanda, G. Peller, and K. Thomas (Eds.), *Critical race theory: The key writings that formed the movement* (pp. 276–291). New York: New Press.

Harris, L. C. (1999). Rethinking the terms of the affirmative action debate established in the Regents of the University of California v. Bakke decision. In P. Batur-Vanderlippe and J. Feagin (Eds.), *The global color line: Racial and ethnic inequality and struggle from a global perspective* (pp. 133–150). Stamford, CT: JAI Press.

Harris, T. M. (2007). Black feminist thought and cultural contracts: Understanding the intersection and negotiation of racial, gendered, and professional identities in the academy. In K. G. Hendrix (Ed.), *Neither white nor male: Female faculty of color* (pp. 25–33). San Francisco: Jossey-Bass.

Hill Collins, P. (2000). *Black feminist thought: Knowledge, consciousness, and the politics of empowerment.* (Rev. ed.). New York: Routledge.

Hubbard, E. E. (2004). *The diversity scorecard: Evaluating the impact of diversity on organizational performance.* Burlington, MA: Elsevier Butterworth-Heinemann.

Huber, G. P. (1991). Organizational learning: The contributing processes and the literatures. *Organization Science, 2*(1), 88–115.

Huffman, M. L. (1995). Organizations, internal labor market policies, and gender inequality in workplace supervisory authority. *Sociological Perspectives, 38*(3), 381–397.

Hurtado, S. (1996). The campus racial climate: Contexts of conflict. In C. S. V. Turner, M. Garcia, A. Nora, and L. I. Redon (Eds.), *Racial and ethnic diversity in higher education* (pp. 485–506). Needham Heights, MA: Simon & Schuster.

Hurtado, S. (2005). The next generation of diversity and intergroup relations research. *Journal of Social Issues, 61*(3), 595–610.

Hurtado, S., Milem, J., Clayton-Pedersen, A., and Allen, W. (1999). Enacting diverse learning environments: Improving the climate for racial/ethnic diversity in higher education. *ASHE-ERIC Higher Education Report*, vol. 26, no. 8. Washington, DC: George Washington University Graduate School of Education and Human Development.

Huselid, M. A., Beatty, R. W., and Becker, B. E. (2005). A players or A positions? The strategic logic of workforce management. *Harvard Business Review, 83*(12), 110–117.

Huy, Q. N. (1999). Emotional capability, emotional intelligence, and radical change. *Academy of Management Review, 24*(2), 325–345.

Huy, Q. N. (2002). Emotional balancing of organizational continuity and radical change: The contribution of middle managers. *Administrative Science Quarterly, 47*(1), 31–69.

Ibarra, H. (1995). Race, opportunity, and diversity of social circles in managerial networks. *Academy of Management Journal, 38*(3), 673–704.

Indiana University. (2005). Mission statement. Retrieved August 3, 2007, from http://www.indiana.edu/~nextpres /mission.shtml.

Indiana University–Purdue University, Indianapolis. (2006). *Through our eyes: The state of the black student at Indiana University Purdue University Indianapolis*. Retrieved January 25, 2009, from http://www.iupui.edu/~divrsity/assets/061102_through_our_eyes.pdf.

Inniss, J. P. (2008). *The politics of double minority status*. Retrieved January 24, 2009, from http://nortonbooks.typepad.com/everydaysociology/2008/07/the-politics-of.html.

Iverson, S. V. (2008). Now is the time for change: Reframing diversity planning at land-grant universities. *Journal of Extension, 46*(1). Retrieved January 23, 2009, from http://www.joe.org/joe/2008february/a3.shtml.

Jackson, J. L., Jr. (2008). *Racial paranoia: The unintended consequences of political correctness: The new reality of race in America*. New York: Basic Civitas.

Jones, R. T. (2005). Liberal education for the twenty-first century: Business expectations. *Liberal Education, 91*(2), 32–37.

Kanov, J. M., and others. (2006). Compassion in organizational life. In J. V. Gallos (Ed.), *Organization development: A Jossey-Bass reader* (pp. 793–812). San Francisco: Jossey-Bass.

Kanter, R. (1991). Globalism/localism: A new human resources agenda. *Harvard Business Review, 69*(2), 9–10.

Kanter, R. (2003). Thriving locally in the global economy. *Harvard Business Review, 81*(8), 119–127.

Kantor, J. (2008, March 14). Beliefs; Pastor's words still draw fire. *New York Times*. Retrieved March 23, 2008, from http://query.nytimes.com/gst/fullpage.html?res=9E07E2DD1238F937A25750C0A96E9C8B63andscp=1andsq=jodi+kantorandst=nyt

Kasparov, G. (2007). *How life imitates chess: Making the right moves—from the board to the boardroom*. New York: Bloomsbury.

Kelly, E. (2006). *Powerful times: Rising to the challenge of our uncertain world.* Upper Saddle River, NJ: Wharton School.

Kent State University, Office of Diversity and Academic Initiatives. (n.d.). *Kent State University strategic diversity plan 2006–2010: Our commitment to inclusive excellence.* Retrieved April 19, 2008, from http://www.kent.edu/diversity/upload/06–2188%20Div%20Strategic%20Plan%203C%20-printed%20and%20final-2.pdf.

Kezar, A. (2000). Pluralistic leadership: Incorporating diverse voices. *Journal of Higher Education, 71*(6), 722–743.

Kezar, A. (2001). Investigating organizational fit in a participatory leadership environment. *Journal of Higher Education Policy and Management, 23*(1), 85–101.

Kezar, A. (2005a). Moving from I to we: Reorganizing for collaboration in higher education. *Change, 37*(6), 50–57.

Kezar, A. (2005b). What campuses need to know about organizational learning and learning organization. In A. Kezar (Ed.), *Organizational learning in higher education* (pp. 7–22). San Francisco: Jossey-Bass.

Kezar, A., Carducci, R., and Contreras-McGavin, M. (2006). Rethinking the "L" word in higher education: The revolution of research on leadership. *ASHE Higher Education Report*, vol. 31, no. 6, San Francisco: Jossey-Bass.

Kezar, A., and Eckel, P. D. (2002). The effect of institutional culture on change strategies in higher education: Universal principles or culturally responsive concepts? *Journal of Higher Education, 73*(4), 435–460.

Kincheloe, J., and Steinberg, D. (1998). Addressing the crisis of whiteness: Reconfiguring white identity in a pedagogy of whiteness. In J. L. Kincheloe, S. R. Steinberg, N. M. Rodriguez, and R. E. Chennault (Eds.), *White reign: Deploying whiteness in America* (pp. 3–29). New York: St. Martin's Press.

King, J., and Gomez, G. G. (2008). *On the pathway to the presidency: Characteristics of higher education's senior leadership.* Washington, DC: American Council on Education.

King, M. L., Jr. (1963). *Letter from a Birmingham jail.* Retrieved August 14, 2008, from http://www.africa.upenn.edu/Articles_Gen/Letter_Birmingham.html.

King, M. L., Jr. (1967). *The world house.* Retrieved August 10, 2008, from http://www.theworldhouse.org/whessay.html.

Kirton, G. (2003). Developing strategic approaches to diversity policy. In M. Davidson and S. L. Fielden (Eds.), *Individual diversity and psychology in organizations* (pp. 3–17). Hoboken, NJ: Wiley.

Knox, M., and Teraguchi, D. H. (2005). Institutional models that cultivate comprehensive change. *Diversity Digest, 9*(2), 10–11.

Kubal, T., Meyler, D., Stone, R. T., and Mauney, T. T. (2003). Teaching diversity and learning outcomes: Bringing lived experience into the classroom. *Teaching Sociology, 31*(4), 441–455.

Kuo, W. H. (1995). Coping with racial discrimination: The case of Asian Americans. *Ethnic and Racial Studies, 18*(1), 109–127.

Kurzweil, R. (2005). *The singularity is near: When humans transcend biology.* London: Penguin Books.

Larkey, L. K. (1996). Toward a theory of communicative interactions in culturally diverse workgroups. *Academy of Management Review, 21*(2), 463–491.

Lawler, E. E. (2006). Business strategy: Creating the winning formula. In J. V. Gallos (Ed.), *Organization development: A Jossey-Bass reader* (pp. 545–564). San Francisco: Jossey-Bass.

Ledford, G. E., Jr. (2002, October). *Attracting, retaining, and motivating employees: The rewards of work framework.* Paper presented at a meeting of the College and University Professional Association for Human Resources, Dallas, TX.

Lee, M. W. (2004). *The art of mindful facilitation.* Berkeley, CA: StirFry Seminars & Consulting.

Lee, S. Y., Florida, R., and Acs, Z. J. (2004). Creativity and entrepreneurship: A regional analysis of new firm formation. *Regional Studies, 38*(8), 879–891.

Legrain, P. (2003). In defense of globalization. *International Economy, 17*(3), 62–65.

Lencioni, P. (2002). *The five dysfunctions of a team: A leadership fable.* San Francisco: Jossey-Bass.

Lin, N. (2001). *Social capital: A theory of social structure and action.* Cambridge, England: Cambridge University Press.

Lindsay, B. (1999). Women chief executives and their approaches towards equity in American universities. *Comparative Education, 35*(2), 187–199.

Lockwood, N. R. (2006, June). *Talent management: Driver for organizational success.* Retrieved January 1, 2008, from http://www.shrm.org/research/quarterly/2006/0606RQuart.asp.

Maher, F. A., and Tetreault, M.K.T. (2007). *Privilege and diversity in the academy.* New York: Routledge.

Mangan, K. (2007). Education dept. will challenge law-school accreditor's diversity standard. *Chronicle of Higher Education, 53*(20), A23.

Mayer, J. D., Salovey, P., and Caruso, D. R. (2004). Emotional intelligence: Theory, findings, and implications. *Psychological Inquiry, 15*(3), 197–215.

Mayhew, M., Grunwald, H., and Dey, E. (2006). Breaking the silence: Achieving a positive campus climate for diversity from the staff perspective. *Research in Higher Education, 47*(1), 63–88.

McCown, B. H. (2008). *Appendix K: Governance leaders' diversity statements, 1997–98.* Retrieved February 1, 2009, from http://www.provost.wisc.edu/plan2008/appendk.html.

McIntosh, P. (n.d.). *White privilege: Unpacking the invisible knapsack.* Retrieved January 21, 2009, from http://www.powervote.org/files/White%20Privilege.pdf.

McRobbie, M. A. (2007). Presidential announcement, board of trustees meeting. Retrieved June 18, 2007, from http://newpres.iu.edu/speeches/030107.shtml.

Meacham, J., and Barrett, C. (2003). Commitment to diversity in institutional mission statements. *Diversity Digest, 7*(1 & 2), 6–7, 9. Retrieved August 3, 2007, from http://www.diversityweb.org/Digest/vol7no1–2/meacham-barrett.cfm.

Michaelson, S. (2007). *Sun Tzu for execution: How to use the art of war to get results.* Avon, MA: Adams Media.

Milem, J. F., Chang, M. J., and Antonio, A. L. (2005). *Making diversity work on campus: A research-based perspective.* Retrieved March 8, 2008, from http://www.aacu.org/inclusive_excellence/documents/Milem_et_al.pdf.

Mittelman, J. H. (1996). The dynamics of globalization. In J. H. Mittelman (Ed.), *Globalization: Critical reflections* (pp. 1–19). Boulder, CO: Lynne Rienner.

Moody, J. (2004). *Faculty diversity: Problems and solutions.* New York: RoutledgeFalmer.

Moses, Y. T. (1997). Black women in academe: Issues and strategies. In L. Benjamin (Ed.), *Black women in the academy: Promises and perils* (pp. 23–38). Gainesville: University Press of Florida.

Muhtaseb, A. (2007). From behind the veil: Students' resistance from different directions. In K. G. Hendrix (Ed.), *Neither white nor male: Female faculty of color* (pp. 25–33). San Francisco: Jossey-Bass.

Musil, C. M. (2006). *Assessing global learning: Matching good intentions with good practice.* Washington, DC: Association of American Colleges and Universities.

Musil, C. M., and others. (1999). *To form a more perfect union: Campus diversity initiatives.* Washington, DC: Association of American Colleges and Universities.

National Association of Diversity Officers in Higher Education. (n.d.). Retrieved August 24, 2008, from http://www.nadohe.org/.

Niemann, Y. F., and Dovidio, J. F. (2005). Affirmative action and job satisfaction: Understanding underlying processes. *Journal of Social Issues, 61*(3), 507–523.

Niemann, Y. F., and Maruyama, G. (2005). Inequities in higher education: Issues and promising practices in a world ambivalent about affirmative action. *Journal of Social Issues, 61*(3), 407–426.

North Carolina State University. (2007a). *NCSU diversity strategic plan.* Retrieved April 18, 2008, from http://www.ncsu.edu/diversity/planning/pdf/RevisedDiversityInitiativeJuly162007.doc.

North Carolina State University. (2007b). *Inclusive excellence: A summary of our strategic plan for achieving authentic diversity.* Retrieved April 18, 2008, from http://www.ncsu.edu/diversity/planning/pdf/SummaryInclusiveExcellencePlan2007.doc.

Not just a glass ceiling. (2008, September 10). *New York Times,* p. A24. Retrieved September 24, 2008, from NewsBank, Inc., database.

Ogletree, C. J., Jr. (2004). *All deliberate speed: Reflections on the first half century of Brown v. Board of Education.* New York: W. W. Norton.

Owen, D. S. (2008). Privileged social identities and diversity leadership in higher education. *Review of Higher Education, 32*(2), 185–207.

Padilla, R. V., and Chávez, R. C. (1995). Introduction. In R. V. Padilla and R. C. Chávez (Eds.), *The leaning ivory tower: Latino professors in American universities* (pp. 1–16). Albany: State University of New York Press.

Patitu, C. L., and Hinton, K. G. (2003). The experiences of African American women faculty and administrators in higher education: Has anything changed? In M. F. Howard-Hamilton (Ed.), *Meeting the needs of African American women.* New directions for student services, no. 104 (pp. 79–84). San Francisco: Jossey-Bass.

Payton, J. (2005). 2005 commencement address. Retrieved July 14, 2007, from http://www.pomona.edu/adwr/president/commencement/05speech.shtml.

Pekow, C. (2006). ABA criticized over diversity mandate at accreditation renewal hearing. *Diverse: Issues in Higher Education, 23*(23), 21. Retrieved April 28, 2008, from the Academic Search Premier database.

Peterson, M. W., and Spencer, M. G. (1990). Understanding academic culture and climate. In W. G. Tierney (Ed.), *Assessing academic climates and cultures* (pp. 3–18). San Francisco: Jossey-Bass.

Pettigrew, T. F. (2004). Justice deferred a half century after Brown v. Board of Education. *American Psychologist, 59*(6), 521–529.

Pettigrew, T. F., and Tropp, L. R. (2006). A meta-analytic test of intergroup contact theory. *Journal of Personality and Social Psychology, 90*(5), 751–783.

Phelps, E. A., and Thomas, L. A. (2003). Race, behavior, and the brain: The role of neuroimaging in understanding complex social behaviors. *Political Psychology, 24*(4), 747–758.

Picca, L. H., and Feagin, J. R. (2007). *Two-faced racism: Whites in the backstage and frontstage*. New York: Routledge.

Powers, E. (2006). *Backlash over student group's demands*. Retrieved January 25, 2009, from http://www.insidehighered.com/news/2006/11/21/iupui.

Prewitt, K. (2002). Demography, diversity, and democracy: The 2000 census story. *Brookings Review, 20*(1), 6–9.

Prilleltensky, I., and Gonick, L. (1994). The discourse of oppression in the social sciences: Past, present, and future. In E. J. Trickett, R. J. Watts, and D. Birman (Eds.), *Human diversity: Perspectives on people in context* (pp. 145–177). San Francisco: Jossey-Bass.

Prilleltensky, I., and Gonick, L. (1996). Politics change, oppression remains: On the psychology and politics of oppression. *Political Psychology, 17*(1), 127–148.

Ragins, B. R. (1995). Diversity, power, and mentorship in organizations: A cultural, structural, and behavioral perspective. In M. M. Chemers, S. Oskamp, and M. Costanzo (Eds.), *Diversity in organizations: New perspectives for a changing workplace* (pp. 91–132). Thousand Oaks, CA: Sage.

Ramaley, J. A. (2006). Governance in a time of transition. In W. G. Tierney (Ed.), *Governance and the public good* (pp. 157–178). Albany: State University of New York Press.

Ridgeway, C. L., and Correll, S. J. (2004). Unpacking the gender system: A theoretical perspective on gender beliefs and social relations. *Gender and Society, 18*(4), 510–531.

Robbins, S. L. (2007). *Teachable moments: Short stories to spark diversity dialogue*. Otsego, MI: PageFree Publishing.

Ropers-Huilman, B. (2008). Women faculty and the dance of identities: Constructing self and privilege within community. In J. Glazer-Raymo (Ed.), *Unfinished agendas: New and continuing gender challenges in higher education* (pp. 35–51). Baltimore: Johns Hopkins University Press.

Ross, E. W., and Gibson, R. (Eds.). (2007). *Neoliberalism and education reform*. Cresskill, NJ: Hampton Press.

St. Jean, Y., and Feagin, J. R. (1998). *Double burden: Black women and everyday racism*. Armonk, NY: M. E. Sharpe.

Sastry, M. A. (1997). Problems and paradoxes in a model of punctuated organizational change. *Administrative Science Quarterly, 42*(2), 237–275.

Schein, E. H. (1992). *Organizational culture and leadership*. San Francisco: Jossey-Bass.

Schein, E. H. (2006). So how can you assess your corporate culture? In J. V. Gallos (Ed.), *Organization development: A Jossey-Bass reader* (pp. 614–633). San Francisco: Jossey-Bass.

Scheurich, J. J., and Young, M. D. (1997). Coloring epistemologies: Are our research epistemologies racially biased? *Educational Researcher, 26*(4), 4–16.

Sedlacek, W. E. (2000). Campus climate surveys: Where to begin. Retrieved August 25, 2007, from http://www.diversityweb.org/Digest/Sp.Sm00/surveys.html.

Selingo, J. J. (2008). A midlife crisis hits college campuses. *Chronicle of Higher Education, 54*(45), B1.

Senge, P. M. (1990). *The fifth discipline: The art and practice of the learning organization.* New York: Doubleday.

Senge, P. M. (2006). The leader's new work: Building learning organizations. In J. V. Gallos (Ed.), *Organization development: A Jossey-Bass reader* (pp. 765–792). San Francisco: Jossey-Bass.

Senge, P. M., and others. (2008). *The necessary revolution: How individuals and organizations are working together to create a sustainable world.* New York: Doubleday.

Shenkar, O. (2006). *The Chinese century: The rising Chinese economy and its impact on the global economy, the balance of power, and your job.* Upper Saddle River, NJ: Wharton School.

Shenkle, C. W., Snyder, R. S., and Bauer, K. W. (1998). Measures of campus climate. In K. W. Buer (Ed.), *Campus climate: Understanding the critical components of today's colleges and universities* (pp. 81–99). San Francisco: Jossey-Bass.

Shockley-Zalabak, P. (2006). *Response to blue ribbon commission on diversity recommendations.* Retrieved September 24, 2007, from https://www.cu.edu/diversity/brc/downloads/presenta _Shockley-Zalabak.pdf.

Silverman, J. (2005). *Plan for diversity at UO stirs controversy on campus.* Retrieved April 19, 2008, from http://www.newsreview.info/article/20050526/NEWS/50526002 /-1/rss01.

Silverman, L. L. (1997). *Organizational architecture: A framework for successful transformation.* Retrieved February 1, 2009, from http://www.partnersforprogress.com/articles/Organizational_Architecture.pdf.

Smith, D. G. (1995). Organizational implications of diversity in higher education. In M. M. Chemers, S. Oskamp, and M. Costanzo (Eds.), *Diversity in organizations: New perspectives for a changing workplace* (pp. 220–244). Thousand Oaks, CA: Sage.

Smith, D. G., and Parker, S. (2005). Organizational learning: A tool for diversity and institutional effectiveness. In A. J. Kezar (Ed.), *Organizational learning in higher education* (pp. 113–126). San Francisco: Jossey-Bass.

Smith, D. G., and Wolf-Wendel, L. (2005). The challenge of diversity: Involvement or alienation in the academy? *ASHE-ERIC Higher Education Report,* vol. 31, no. 1 (Rev. ed.), San Francisco: Jossey-Bass.

Smith, P. J., and Sadler-Smith, E. (2006). *Learning in organizations: Complexities and diversities.* London: Routledge.

Society for Human Resource Management. (2008). Retrieved August 24, 2008, from http://www.shrm.org/kc/.

Solorzano, D., Ceja, M., and Yosso, T. (2000). Critical race theory, racial microaggressions, and campus racial climate: The experiences of African American college students. *Journal of Negro Education, 69*(1/2), 60–73.

Spanier, G. B., and Baldwin, C. (2004). *The structure of public boards does matter.* Retrieved August 10, 2008, from http://president.psu.edu/editorials/articles/structurematters.html.

Spreitzer, G. M. (1995). Psychological empowerment in the workplace: Dimensions, measurement and validation. *Academy of Management Journal, 38*(5), 1442–1465.

Spreitzer, G. M. (1996). Social structural characteristics of psychological empowerment. *Academy of Management Journal, 39*(2), 483–504.

Spreitzer, G. M., de Janasz, S. C., and Quinn, R. E. (1999). Empowered to lead: The role of psychological empowerment in leadership. *Journal of Organizational Behavior, 20*(4), 511–526.

State University of New York, Stony Brook. (2005). *Stony Brook University campus climate survey report: 2004–05.* Retrieved September 23, 2007, from http://ws.cc.stonybrook.edu/diversity/images/documents/Taskforce_files/ccs2004results.pdf.

State University of New York, Stony Brook. (2006). *Draft report and action plan of the president's task force on campus climate.* Retrieved September 23, 2007, from http://www.sunysb.edu/diversity/images/documents/campus_climate_report/ccr2006.pdf.

Stern, G. J. (1999). *The Drucker Foundation self-assessment tool: Process guide.* (Rev. ed.). San Francisco: Jossey-Bass.

Stiglitz, J. E. (2006). *Making globalization work.* New York: W. W. Norton.

Sull, D. N. (2002). *Why good companies go bad. In Harvard business review on culture and change* (pp. 83–106). Boston: Harvard Business School Press.

Sullivan, L. G., Reichard, D., and Shumate, D. (2005). Using campus climate surveys to foster participatory governance. *Community College Journal of Research and Practice, 29*(6), 427–443.

Tannen, D. (1994). *Talking from 9 to 5: Women and men at work.* New York: Harper.

Tapia, R. A. (2007). True diversity doesn't come from abroad. *Chronicle of Higher Education, 54*(5), B34–35. Retrieved October 14, 2007, from http://chronicle.com/weekly/v54/i05/05b03401.htm.

Tedlow, R. S. (2008). Leaders in denial. *Harvard Business Review, 86*(7/8), 18–19.

Thiederman, S. B. (2003). *Making diversity work: Seven steps for defeating bias in the workplace.* Chicago: Dearborn Trade.

Thomas, D. A. (1993). Racial dynamics in cross-race developmental relationships. *Administrative Science Quarterly, 38*(2), 169–194.

Thomas, D. A. (2006). Diversity as strategy. In J. V. Gallos (Ed.), *Organization development: A Jossey-Bass reader* (pp. 748–764). San Francisco: Jossey-Bass.

Thomas, D. A., and Ely, R. J. (1996). Making differences matter: A new paradigm for managing diversity. *Harvard Business Review, 74*(5), 79–90.

Thomas, K. W., and Velthouse, B. A. (1990). Cognitive elements of empowerment: An "interpretive" model of intrinsic task motivation. *Academy of Management Review, 15*(4), 666–681.

Thomas, R. R., Jr. (1990). From affirmative action to affirming diversity. *Harvard Business Review, 90*(2), 107–117.

Thomas, R. R., Jr. (2006). *Building on the promise of diversity: How we can move to the next level in our workplaces, our communities, and our society.* New York: AMACOM.

Timmons, H. (2007, December 13). India, a stirring giant, is the new place to see and be seen. *New York Times,* p. C1. Retrieved January 1, 2008, from the NewsBank, Inc., database.

Toffler, A. (1970). *Future shock.* New York: Random House.

Tromski, D., and Doston, G. (2003). Interactive drama: A method for experiential multicultural training. *Journal of Multicultural Counseling and Development, 31*(1), 52–62.

Tsui, A. S., Egan, T. D., and Xin, K. R. (1995). Diversity in organizations: Lessons from demography research. In M. M. Chemers, S. Oskamp, and M. Costanzo (Eds.), *Diversity in organizations: New perspectives for a changing workplace* (pp. 191– 219). Thousand Oaks, CA: Sage.

Turner, C.S.V. (2002). *Diversifying the faculty: A guidebook for search committees.* Washington, DC: Association of American Colleges and Universities.

Turner, C.S.V., Myers, S. L., Samuel, L., and Creswell, J. W. (1999). Exploring underrepresentation: The case of faculty of color in the Midwest. *Journal of Higher Education, 70*(1), 27–45.

Tushman, M. L., and Romaneli, E. (1985). Organizational evolution: A metamorphosis model of convergence and reorientation. In L. L. Cummings and B. M. Staw (Eds.). *Research in Organizational Behavior* Vol. 7 (171–222). Greenwich, CT: JAI Press.

Ulrich, D. (1998a). Intellectual capital = competence × commitment. *Sloan Management Review, 39*(2), 15–26.

Ulrich, D. (1998b). A new mandate for human resources. *Harvard Business Review, 76*(1), 124–134.

Ulrich, D., Brockbank, W., Johnson, D., and Younger, J. (2007). *Human resource competencies: Responding to increased expectations.* Retrieved March 5, 2009 from www.interscience.wiley.com.

Ulrich, D., and Creelman, D. (2006). In touch with intangibles. *Workforce Management, 85*(9), 38–42.

Ulrich, D., and Smallwood, N. (2003). *Why the bottom line isn't! How to build value through people and organization.* San Francisco: Jossey-Bass.

Ulrich, D., and Smallwood, N. (2004). Capitalizing on capabilities. *Harvard Business Review, 82*(6), 119–127.

University of Michigan: Diversity blueprints final report. (2007). Retrieved September 14, 2007, from University of Michigan, Diversity: Research and Resources Web site: http://www.vpcomm.umich.edu/diversityresources/db-summary.html.

University of Oregon: Progress reporting guidelines diversity strategic action plans 2007–2008 academic year. (n.d.). Retrieved April 19, 2008, from University of Oregon, Office of Institutional Equity and Diversity Web site: http://vpdiversity.uoregon.edu/SAP_Progress_reporting_document.doc.

The University of Vermont: Strategic plan performance indicators fall, 2007. (2007). Retrieved April 18, 2008, from The University of Vermont, Office of the President Web site: http://www.uvm.edu/~presdent/strategic_planning/SPPI_Metrics _FINAL.pdf.

U.S. Department of Education, National Center for Education Statistics. (2005). *Integrated Postsecondary Education Data Survey, Fall Staff Survey 2005.* Analysis by the American Council on Education.

U.S. Department of Education, National Center for Education Statistics, Integrated Postsecondary Education System (IPEDS). (2007). *Change in enrollment by race at public research universities between fall 1994 and 2004.* Analysis by the American Council on Education.

U.S. Department of Labor, Employment Standards Administration. (2007). *Office of federal contract compliance programs.* Retrieved August 11, 2007, from http://www.dol.gov/esa/ofccp/.

University of California. (2006). *The representation of minorities among ladder rank faculty: Report of the UC president's task force on faculty diversity.* Retrieved December 29, 2007, from http://www.universityofcalifornia.edu/facultydiversity/report.pdf.

University of California. (2007). *Study group on university diversity campus climate report.* Retrieved December 29, 2007, from http://www.universityofcalifornia.edu/diversity/documents/07-campus_report.pdf.

University of California, Davis. (2003). *The principles of community.* Retrieved May 19, 2008, from http://principles.ucdavis.edu/default.html.

University of California, Davis. (2007). *Diversity education series.* Retrieved October 7, 2007, from http://diversity.ucdavis.edu/education.cfm.

University of California, Irvine. (2007). *Our mission as a public research university. III. Diversity, access and financial aid.* Retrieved August 3, 2007, from http://www.strategicplan.uci.edu/?p=21.

University of California, Los Angeles. (2005). *Academic personnel manual: Appointment and promotion. Review and appraisal committees.* Retrieved December 29, 2007, from http://www.faculty.diversity.ucla.edu/03recruit/committee/stk/docs/apm-210.pdf.

University of California, Los Angeles. (2006). *Institutional proposal to the Western Association of Schools and Colleges.* Retrieved July 20, 2008, from http://www.wasc.ucla.edu/UCLA-Institutional-Proposal-to-WASC.pdf.

University of Illinois at Urbana-Champaign, Center on Democracy in a Multiracial Society. (2002). *Mission statement.* Retrieved April 27, 2008, from http://cdms.ds.uiuc.edu/Home_Page.htm.

University of Toronto. (2006). *A green paper for public discussion describing the characteristics of the best (public) research universities.* Retrieved April 18, 2008, from http://www.provost.utoronto.ca/Assets/assets/green2.pdf?method=1.

University of Washington, University Diversity Council. (2009). *About the diversity council.* Retrieved February 1, 2009, from http://www.washington.edu/diversity/divcoun/index.html.

University of Wisconsin–Madison. (2007). *Tools for effective leaders.* Retrieved August 29, 2007, from http://www.provost.wisc.edu/climate/leadertools.html.

Valentine, V. (2003). Questions: John Payton on affirmative action. *The Crisis, 110*(4), 9.

Valverde, L. A. (2003). *Leaders of color in higher education: Unrecognized triumphs in harsh institutions.* Walnut Creek, CA: AltaMira Press.

van Dick, R., and others. (2004). Role of perceived importance in intergroup contact. *Journal of Personality and Social Psychology, 87*(2), 211–227.

vanden Heuvel, K. (2008). *Transformational presidency.* Retrieved January 25, 2009, from http://www.thenation.com/blogs/edcut/380292.

Visconti, L. (2007, April). Keynote address. Speech presented at the meeting of the American Association of Affirmative Action, Austin, Texas.

Watson, J. (2008). When diversity training goes awry. *Diverse: Issues in Higher Education, 24*(25), 11–13. Retrieved April 2, 2008, from http://www.diverseeducation.com/artman/publish/article_10543.shtml.

Wesolowski, M. A., and Mossholder, K. W. (1997). Relational demography in supervisor-subordinate dyads: Impact on subordinate job satisfaction, burnout, and perceived procedural justice. *Journal of Organizational Behavior, 18*(4), 351–362.

Western Association of Schools and Colleges. (2001). *Handbook of accreditation.* Retrieved May 21, 2008, from http://www.wascsenior.org/wasc/PDFs/080311_Updated. 2001. Handbook.for.web.pdf.

White, J., and Weathersby, R. (2005). Can universities become true learning organizations? *Learning Organization, 12*(3), 292–298.

Williams, D. A., Berger, J. B., and McClendon, S. A. (2005). *Toward a model of inclusive excellence and change in postsecondary institutions.* Washington, DC: Association of American Colleges and Universities.

Williams, D. A., and Wade-Golden, K. C. (2007a). The chief diversity officer. *CUPA-HR Journal, 58*(1), 40–49.

Williams, D. A., and Wade-Golden, K. C. (2007b). *The chief diversity officer: A primer for college and university presidents.* Washington, DC: American Council on Education.

Wise, T. (2008a). *Of national lies and racial amnesia: Jeremiah Wright, Barack Obama, and the audacity of truth.* Retrieved March 23, 2008, from http://www.lipmagazine.org/%7Etimwise/NationalLies.html.

Wise, T. (2008b). *White like me: Reflections on race from a privileged son.* (Rev. ed.). Brooklyn, NY: Soft Skull Press.

Yeung, A. K., Ulrich, D. O., Nason, S. W., and Von Glinow, M. A. (1999). *Organizational learning capability: Generating and generalizing ideas with impact.* Oxford, England: Oxford University Press.

Yoder, J. D. (1991). Rethinking tokenism: Looking beyond numbers. *Gender and Society, 5*(2), 178–192.

Yosso, T. J., Parker, L., Solorzano, D. G., and Lynn, M. (2004). From Jim Crow to affirmative action and back again: A critical race discussion of racialized rationales and access to higher education. *Review of Research in Education, 28,* 1–25.

Zakaria, F. (2008). *The post-American world.* New York: W.W. Norton.

Zúñiga, X., Nagda, B. A., Chesler, M., and Cytron-Walker, A. (2007). *Intergroup dialogue in higher education: Meaningful learning about social justice.* San Francisco: Jossey-Bass.

Name Index

Collins, J. C., 32
Contreras–McGavin, M., 47
Cooper, J., 4
Cordova, D. I., 47
Correll, S. J., 8
Cox, T., Jr., 61, 75
Creelman, D., 16
Crenshaw, K., 6
Creswell, J. W., 80
Crocker, J., 77
Crosby, F. J., 43
Crossan, M., 53
Crowfoot, J. E., 54, 97, 98
Cruz, D. M., 21
Cudd, A. E., 5
Cytron–Walker, A., 76, 100

D

Darlington, P.S.E., 7
Davis–LaMastro, V., 78
de Janasz, S. C., 26
Dees, M., 82
Delgado, R., 6
Denison, D. R., 92
Detert, J. R., 92
Devine, P. G., 72
Dey, E., 58
Digh, P., 54
Dipboye, R. L., 70
Doston, G., 83
Dovidio, J. F., 8, 69, 70, 71, 73, 74, 76, 80
Drucker, P. F., 19

E

Easterby–Smith, M., 53
Eckel, P. D., 47, 54, 71
Edmondson, A. C., 102, 103
Egan, T. D., 39
Ehrich, L. C., 80
Eisenberger, R., 78
Eisenhardt, K. M., 68
Eisenstat, R. A., 81, 101, 102
Ely, R. J., 71, 75, 103
Evans, A., 2, 3, 6, 20, 34, 43, 49, 62, 77
Ezeamii, H. C., 89, 90

F

Fain, P., 45
Farrell, E. F., 33
Fasolo, P., 78
Feagin, J. R., 1, 5, 8, 9, 13, 18, 23, 55, 72, 84, 105
Fegley, S., 63
Feldman, J., 82
Fenelon, J., 49
Firebaugh, F. M., 10
Fletcher, M. A., 1, 2, 5
Florida, R., 11, 12, 16, 17, 20, 33, 34, 64
Foley, J., 41, 56
Ford, R. T., 30, 31
Freire, P., 22
Friedman, T. L., 11, 12
Frohnmayer, D., 82
Fullan, M., 67, 68, 70, 71, 72, 73, 87, 100

G

Gaertner, S. L., 9, 69, 70, 74
Gappa, J. M., 18, 19
Garcia, M., 59
Gibson, R., 13
Girves, J. E., 80
Glynn, M. A., 70
Gomez, G. G., 2, 47
Gonick, L., 3, 6, 21, 22, 44, 77
Gonzalez, M. C., 21
Goodnight, J., 16
Gose, B., 82
Gotanda, N., 6
Graham, S., 35
Greenberg, J., 82
Gregersen, H. B., 53, 73
Grossman, R. J., 61
Grunwald, H., 58
Gwathmey, J. K., 80

H

Hamel, G., 28, 33, 48
Hamilton, N. W., 40, 45
Hansen, H. K., 11
Hansford, B., 80

Subject Index

A

Accountability: avoidance of, 87; creating measures of, 81, 85

Accreditation: as external impetus for change, 88; measuring internal change progress through, 88–91

Accrediting Council for Independent Colleges and Schools, 91

Active inertia, 69

Affirmative action: board of trustees support of, 46; court decisions on educational equality and, 29–31, 82, 88; Executive Order 11246 on, 42–43, 82

American Psychological Association, 76

"American tapestry," 10

Association of American Colleges and Universities, 32

Association of Governing Boards of Universities and Colleges, 45

B

Bakke, Regents of the University of California, 29, 30

Berlin Wall (1989), 11, 31

Bias: definition of, 69; reducing levels of intergroup, 74

Board of trustees: description and duties of, 44–45; diversity leadership by, 45–46

Bollinger, Gratz v., 27, 29

Bollinger, Grutter v., 29, 30

Bradley, Milliken v., 31

Brown v. Board of Education, 30–31, 82

C

California State University Board of Trustees, 45

Campus climate: culture and, 56–57; methods of cultural assessment of, 57–58; studies on, 58–60

Campus Diversity Initiative (California), 38, 40, 49, 52

CBS News, 5

Center on Democracy in a Multiracial Society (University of Illinois), 55

Chief diversity officer (CDO), 50

China, 12–13

Chronicle of Higher Education, 54

Circle Project, 54

Civil rights movement, 82–83

Civil War, 2

Cognitive dissonance, 69

Coker v. Georgia, 82

Collaborative on Academic Careers in Higher Education, 59, 64

Common identity, 74

Communication: democratized technology facilitating, 11; diversity strategic focus on discourses and, 49–50

Conversation (*convertere*), 95

Creative capital: demography, diversity, and democracy framework for attracting, 18–21; description, 16; facilitated by psychological empowerment, 26; research university ability to attract, 17–18; talent management of, 31–35

About the Authors

Edna Chun is vice president for human resources and equity at Broward College in Fort Lauderdale, Florida, a large urban community college with four campuses and sixty thousand students. In this capacity, she oversees recruitment, staffing, diversity and affirmative action, employee and labor relations, compensation, records management, and benefits administration. She has more than two decades of human resource experience in public research universities in the California, Oregon, and Ohio state university systems. Chun holds doctor of music and master of music degrees with high distinction from Indiana University, a master of arts degree from the Columbia University Graduate School of Arts and Sciences, and a bachelor of arts degree cum laude from Oberlin College. She is a frequent presenter at national and regional conferences on diversity and affirmative action.

Alvin Evans is associate vice president for human resources at Kent State University, a doctoral extensive university with eight campuses. He has more than twenty years of experience in public sector human resource administration and organizational development. At Kent State, he oversees a broad range of functions, including recruitment and staffing, labor relations, and benefits. Evans served as a Distinguished Fellow for the Department of Health, Education, and Welfare.

Evans holds a bachelor of arts degree in history and government from Benedict College, a master of education degree in history and social studies from South Carolina State University. His educational background also includes doctoral studies in history, government, and international studies at the University of South Carolina. He is a frequent presenter and panelist at national and regional conferences on talent management and diversity.

Chun and Evans received the prestigious Francis G. Hansen Publication Award from the College and University Professional Association for Human Resources for their recent monograph, *Are the Walls Really Down? Behavioral and Organizational Barriers to Faculty and Staff Diversity* (Jossey-Bass, 2007). They have coauthored a number of articles on talent management and institutional diversity strategies.

About the ASHE Higher Education Report Series

Since 1983, the ASHE (formerly ASHE-ERIC) Higher Education Report Series has been providing researchers, scholars, and practitioners with timely and substantive information on the critical issues facing higher education. Each monograph presents a definitive analysis of a higher education problem or issue, based on a thorough synthesis of significant literature and institutional experiences. Topics range from planning to diversity and multiculturalism, to performance indicators, to curricular innovations. The mission of the Series is to link the best of higher education research and practice to inform decision making and policy. The reports connect conventional wisdom with research and are designed to help busy individuals keep up with the higher education literature. Authors are scholars and practitioners in the academic community. Each report includes an executive summary, review of the pertinent literature, descriptions of effective educational practices, and a summary of key issues to keep in mind to improve educational policies and practice.

The Series is one of the most peer reviewed in higher education. A National Advisory Board made up of ASHE members reviews proposals. A National Review Board of ASHE scholars and practitioners reviews completed manuscripts. Six monographs are published each year and they are approximately 120 pages in length. The reports are widely disseminated through Jossey-Bass and John Wiley & Sons, and they are available online to subscribing institutions through Wiley InterScience (http://www.interscience.wiley.com).

Call for Proposals

The ASHE Higher Education Report Series is actively looking for proposals. We encourage you to contact one of the editors, Dr. Kelly Ward (kaward@wsu.edu) or Dr. Lisa Wolf-Wendel (lwolf@ku.edu), with your ideas.

Recent Titles

ASHE HIGHER EDUCATION REPORT
Order Form
SUBSCRIPTIONS AND SINGLE ISSUES

DISCOUNTED BACK ISSUES:

*Use this form to receive **20% off** all back issues of ASHE Higher Education Report. All single issues priced at **$23.20** (normally $29.00)*

TITLE	ISSUE NO.	ISBN
_____	_____	_____
_____	_____	_____
_____	_____	_____

*Call **888-378-2537** or see mailing instructions below. When calling, mention the promotional code, JB7ND, to receive your discount.*

SUBSCRIPTIONS: *(1 year, 6 issues)*

☐ New Order   ☐ Renewal

U.S.	☐ Individual: $174	☐ Institutional: $228
Canada/Mexico	☐ Individual: $174	☐ Institutional: $288
All Others	☐ Individual: $210	☐ Institutional: $339

*Call **888-378-2537** or see mailing and pricing instructions below. Online subscriptions are available at www.interscience.wiley.com.*

Copy or detach page and send to:
John Wiley & Sons, Journals Dept., 5th Floor
989 Market Street, San Francisco, CA 94103-1741

Order Form can also be faxed to: 888-481-2665

Issue/Subscription Amount: $ _____	**SHIPPING CHARGES:**
Shipping Amount: $ _____	SURFACE Domestic Canadian
(for single issues only—subscription prices include shipping)	First Item $5.00 $6.00
Total Amount: $ _____	Each Add'l Item $3.00 $1.50

(No sales tax for U.S. subscriptions. Canadian residents, add GST for subscription orders. Individual rate subscriptions must be paid by personal check or credit card. Individual rate subscriptions may not be resold as library copies.)

☐ Payment enclosed (U.S. check or money order only. All payments must be in U.S. dollars.)

☐ VISA ☐ MC ☐ Amex # _____ Exp. Date _____

Card Holder Name _____ Card Issue # _____

Signature _____ Day Phone _____

☐ Bill Me (U.S. institutional orders only. Purchase order required.)

Purchase order # _____
                   Federal Tax ID13559302   GST 89102 8052

Name _____

Address _____

Phone _____ E-mail _____

JB7ND

ASHE-ERIC HIGHER EDUCATION REPORT
IS NOW AVAILABLE ONLINE AT WILEY INTERSCIENCE

What is Wiley InterScience?

Wiley InterScience is the dynamic online content service from John Wiley & Sons delivering the full text of over 300 leading scientific, technical, medical, and professional journals, plus major reference works, the acclaimed Current Protocols laboratory manuals, and even the full text of select Wiley print books online.

What are some special features of Wiley InterScience?

Wiley Interscience Alerts is a service that delivers table of contents via e-mail for any journal available on Wiley InterScience as soon as a new issue is published online.

Early View is Wiley's exclusive service presenting individual articles online as soon as they are ready, even before the release of the compiled print issue. These articles are complete, peer-reviewed, and citable.

CrossRef is the innovative multi-publisher reference linking system enabling readers to move seamlessly from a reference in a journal article to the cited publication, typically located on a different server and published by a different publisher.

How can I access Wiley InterScience?

Visit http://www.interscience.wiley.com.

Guest Users can browse Wiley InterScience for unrestricted access to journal Tables of Contents and Article Abstracts, or use the powerful search engine.

Registered Users are provided with a *Personal Home Page* to store and manage customized alerts, searches, and links to favorite journals and articles. Additionally, Registered Users can view free Online Sample Issues and preview selected material from major reference works.

Licensed Customers are entitled to access full-text journal articles in PDF, with select journals also offering full-text HTML.

How do I become an Authorized User?

Authorized Users are individuals authorized by a paying Customer to have access to the journals in Wiley InterScience. For example, a University that subscribes to Wiley journals is considered to be the Customer.

Faculty, staff and students authorized by the University to have access to those journals in Wiley InterScience are Authorized Users. Users should contact their Library for information on which Wiley journals they have access to in Wiley InterScience.

ASK YOUR INSTITUTION ABOUT WILEY INTERSCIENCE TODAY!